W9-AUM-490

The Hills of
CHIANTI

The Hills of
CHIANTI

The Story of a Tuscan Winemaking Family,
in Seven Bottles

—— PIERO ANTINORI ——

Translated by Natalie Danford

Published in the United States of America in 2014
By Rizzoli Ex Libris, an imprint of
Rizzoli International Publications, Inc.
300 Park Avenue South
New York, NY 10010
www.rizzoliusa.com

Originally published in Italy as Il Profumo del Chianti
Copyright © 2013 Arnoldo Mondadori Editore S.p.A. Milano
Translation Copyright © 2014 Natalie Danford

2014 2015 2016 2017 / 10 9 8 7 6 5 4 3 2 1

Distributed in the U.S. trade by Random House, New York
Printed in U.S.A.

ISBN-13: 978-0-8478-4388-6
Library of Congress Catalog Control Number: 2014935607

CONTENTS

The Hills of
CHIANTI

PROLOGUE

Two small girls run through the fields under a Chianti sunset, hold-ing between them a basket filled to the rim with grapes. They've been keeping a watchful eye on the thick vines at the end of the field, which grow twisted tightly around an old tree. Tuscans would call those vines "married." In late 1979, when the grown-ups were tending to the new vineyard, those girls begged for a plot of land of their own. "Can we make wine, Dad? Please?" they asked, and then asked again, and then again. Finally, I relented.

It's their late autumn game in the fields around our coun-try house. It's not an easy game, either. Those grapes have to be destemmed, cleaned, pressed, and then transferred into vats. And then comes the waiting. When it's finally time, they bottle that wine in a dozen Bordeaux bottles. They design a label of their own and introduce the wine at a dinner in the city. Around the table are our closest friends, including a nice man who spends so many evenings discussing barriques and terroir with me.

Grapes have been harvested in those hills in September for more than two thousand years—as many as ten thousand years, according to *Vitis vinifera* fossils discovered in the area. But that small, playful harvest was special in my eyes. That vineyard is called Tignanello, and it wends its way up a slope between the Greve and Pesa Valleys, south of Florence. By 1979, it had produced just a few vintages of a red that was much discussed in Tuscany and around the world. The vineyard that was the playground of those two girls had only recently begun to produce Solaia, a red that *Wine Spectator* magazine would one day call the best wine in the world. And those two girls were my daughters Albiera and Allegra. The dinner was actually the launch for Tignanello, and it was held in Palazzo Antinori in Piazza Antinori in Florence. And the nice man, who wrote books and spoke about wine and food on television and who would write about my daughters' earliest attempt at winemaking, was Luigi Veronelli, a pacesetter, a critic, a creative thinker, a poet of the nectar of Bacchus, who told the world about the fantastic new Italian wines. You might even say that he started a whole movement.

Today, Albiera is vice president of Antinori. Twenty years after she and her sister made their wine, she ran into Veronelli at Vinitaly, the wine fair in Verona. He held one of those famous bottles in his hand.

"That's probably not even good vinegar by now," she told him, smiling.

"We'll never know," he answered. "It's so precious to me that I've never had the heart to open it!" The father of the new culture of Italian wine, who passed away in 2004, understood that something important and new was fermenting in my daughters' bottles. Though at the end of the most difficult half century in the history of the company that bears my name, it seemed like the proverbial glass was more than half empty, everything was actually about to begin.

1

MONTENISA BRUT ROSÉ

Sowing the Future

*I*f I had to choose just one wine to represent my daughters, it would be a Montenisa sparkling wine. More specifically, a Franciacorta Brut Rosé, one of our more recent additions.

Albiera, Allegra, and Alessia—my three daughters—are the modern international soul of Marchesi Antinori. They spent their childhoods in the ancient rooms of Palazzo Antinori; today their offices are located there. All three have lives that revolve around planes, trains, and international events.

The oldest, Albiera, Antinori's vice president, travels to Asia frequently. The brains behind Antinori marketing and an expert in architecture, Albiera created our farm-stay inn at Fonte de' Medici. She's currently helping to create our new winery in Bargino, in the San Casciano Val di Pesa area. She's also adeptly handled the challenge of being the Florentine female president of a traditional Piedmont winemaker, Prunotto. She confessed, "When I got there

I wasn't yet thirty years old. I knew nothing about the Nebbiolo grape, and the enologist had to translate the dialect that the growers spoke for me!"

Allegra, who handles public relations, nurtures a passion for the restaurant side of the business. Among her many successes, she established Cantinetta Antinori branches in Vienna, Moscow, and Zurich.

Alessia is the youngest and the daughter who most strongly resembles her grandfather Niccolò, according to my friends. Alessia has pored over tomes about winemaking since she was a little girl, and now she's our enologist. She's overseen production at Montenisa for years, but she also handles exports to the United States and emerging markets. In 2003 she had the great honor of serving as president of the organization Primum Familiae Vini, the United Nations of historic wine families.

These days, Italian winemaking magazines and lots of other publications love interviewing my daughters—indeed, the three of them get more press than I do. Sometimes they're interviewed individually, and sometimes as a group. Their faces, their voices, and their Tuscan accents grace thousands of video clips. They've appeared over and over, talking about this or that wine or the harvest at one of our Tuscan or Californian vineyards. Their words have been translated into dozens of different languages. In early 2011, *Newsweek* included them in a list of fifteen iconic Italian women not "celebrated simply for their cleavage or for their ability to make a big, comforting Sunday dinner."

Each bottle of Montenisa is labeled with a logo of three entwined A's on a white background meant to celebrate the teamwork of these three winemakers. My daughters may share the same last name and first initial, but they have distinct personalities and work styles. Allegra is enthusiastic and outgoing. Alessia is demonstrative and decisive. Like every big sister, Albiera is the mediator who makes peace between her younger siblings. The older two were brought up with a stricter hand—they were monitored closely by nannies and had to obey a curfew. By the time the youngest came along, times had changed, so she was raised a little more freely. She attended college and began traveling earlier than her sisters had. Each is unique, but together they have a special way of smoothing over differences and finding a way for each person to contribute. They dreamed up, independently produced, and brought to market this new wine—an intense and complex Franciacorta with the kind of fascinating history that exists behind every good wine. "Every wine tells a story," as Veronelli once wrote.

This wine's vineyard is named for a mountain beloved by Bacchus. It stands in the heart of Franciacorta in the Lombardy region, south of Lake Iseo. Making wine in this area was a new challenge. We didn't know how exporting our age-old history so far from its Tuscan roots would work out. However, there was a powerful motivation—we wanted Antinori to be involved in sparkling wine again. Technically speaking, Tuscan grapes aren't varieties that are normally used to produce high-quality sparkling wine. The *perlage*, the bubbles, the image, and the spirit of traditional Tuscan wines all combine to make them members of a tribe with substance and personality. Their feet are planted firmly on the ground, and they demonstrate little interest in or aptitude for frivolous fizz. Or at least that's what we used to think, but a company that wants to grow and endure must always take new roads and push against traditional boundaries.

My grandfather Piero Antinori was the first to attempt to make a Tuscan version of Champagne—a legendary wine of joy and celebration. This was back in the prehistoric era of Italian winemaking. He was traveling through the vineyards of France in search of inspiration, and he'd brought along a few bottles of the best white from Cigliano, one of our first Tuscan vineyards. In Marne, in Épernay, the capital of Champagne, the staff of an enological institute tasted it and discussed the magic of bubbles. (Even the concept of an enological institute was a novelty to my grandfather; there were no wine academies in Italy at the time.) In the end, the wine was judged to have potential. In 1904, the first Gran Spumante Marchese Antinori was made. After the Ferrari family, makers of Italy's sparking wine *par excellence,* we were the second in Italy to attempt to employ the *méthode Champenoise.* The results were satisfying and puzzling in equal measure.

So-called champagne from Chianti (our area of Tuscany, which was already known for red wine by then) began to crop up on the wine lists of famous restaurants and menus for dinners at the Quirinale in Rome, where the kings of Italy raised glasses full of it. Even the great musician Giacomo Puccini loved it. In 1914, he wrote a letter (my father kept it safely stowed in a desk drawer for years) inquiring about our "aristocratic" sparkling wine. It was called "Cordon Rouge" at the time. But sparkling wine is cantankerous. One morning several years later, about seven thousand bottles exploded over the course of a few hours, making a sound like heavy-artillery fire as they shattered all over the San Casciano wine cellars. The French expert my family had called in specifically to oversee that wine had made a grave mistake (and was swiftly sent packing). Workers had to don fencing masks to go in and clean up the scene of the "shoot-out."

This legendary wizard of Champagne, Charlemagne (his name even sounds like the name of the grape), apparently had made an error in the *tirage, remuage,* or *dégorgement,* the then-mysterious phases of fermentation used to create that special wine. At the time, some ventured that he'd merely been nostalgic for his days fighting in the trenches for the French army during World War I. Whatever the reason behind this disaster, one thing is certain: my father argued so vociferously with my grandfather over sparkling wine— my father wanted to continue trying to make it, despite the dangerous outcome—that the two almost came to blows. Eventually my father applied for a bank loan, took out another loan from a relative, moved production into a different area, in San Martino alla Palma, and hired a new winemaker from France. Unlike his predecessor, the new winemaker, Granvalet, proved to be worth his salt. We Antinoris don't give up easily. And we still make sparkling wines. In fact, years after those early efforts with bubbles, today we're one of the top producers of high-quality Italian sparkling wines. In 1975 we were among the ten companies that founded the Istituto Italiano Spumante Classico–Méthode Champenoise.

New times call for new parameters. In the late 1990s, my daughters and I began to look for land where we could grow grapes for high-quality sparkling wine to mark our one hundredth anniversary making it. We found the ideal land in an enchanting corner of Lombardy, between the lake and the mountains. The vineyard is surrounded by a *brolo,* an old garden wall, near a small town with a smattering of medieval churches and a fifteenth-century villa. It was love at first sight. The search proved my theory that a good winemaker and his vineyard will always find each other. I've always believed that the best wines are made in tranquil places rich in history and personality. That beauty finds its way into the bottle. This humble piece of land was even located in traditional sparkling wine territory. It was perfect.

In order to grow grapes in an area that had a wine culture and tradition so different from our own, we formed a partnership in 1999 with an old and noble Brescia family: the Maggi counts. They're an eclectic bunch. The first owner of that land, Aymo, loved sparkling wines and fast cars in equal measure. He was one of the founders of the Mille Miglia automobile endurance race that was run on the open road in the 1920s. Today, Alessia gets along famously with the youngest generation of the family. Great wines always rely on a network of contacts, cooperation, and friendships. Those things are fundamental, especially when planting and harvesting far from home. The Maggis still own the land, but we were given carte blanche to start producing wine there again. Albiera, Allegra, and Alessia demonstrated their vocation for the land by planting new vines and reestablishing the winery. Then, they waited.

An Antinori sisters' wine. To understand how much that means, you have to go back a little to the early 1980s, when such a thing seemed impossible. It was a tough time, and things were precarious. My sister, Ilaria, and my brother, Lodovico, had left the company. She wasn't interested in the world of wine, and he had other projects he wanted to pursue. The exit of two family members had placed the Antinori brand in a difficult spot financially. I was racked by worry that our family's illustrious history might be drawing to a close, not just for business reasons, but for personal reasons as well.

Today, I'd be among the first to insist that men and women have the same strengths and abilities, in wine as elsewhere. Indeed, there's been something of a women's revolution in the Italian wine world. Think of Gaia Gaja, daughter of Angelo (he had fun coming up with that name for her!), who has been so successful with that label, which is famous for reds from Piedmont. In Sicily, Francesca Planeta and José Rallo from the Donnafugata family are already part of the second generation of female winemakers. Then there are the Lungarotti sisters in Umbria, Elisabetta Foradori in Trentino, and many other excellent and enthusiastic women winemakers. Many of them are members of the Associazione Nazionale Le Donne del Vino, an entire trade group of female winemakers. I think soon women in Italy will earn their rightful place in society and in business, and no special treatment will be needed to ensure equality.

But I have to admit, thirty years ago I wasn't so enlightened. I couldn't have imagined that one day my three young daughters would be involved in making wine and growing grapes, or that they'd be negotiating with people all over the world. The world of wine, as cosmopolitan as it might be—and there's no denying that people who work in wine are passionate about their work and truly live and breathe wine—was not terribly open to change. I'm talking about what's in the bottles, but also what goes on outside the bottles. I know more than a little about the subject.

Looking back through the Antinori family history my father wrote toward the end of his life, I did find a mention of one woman who played a key role—in 1385. This was a time when the best wine in the world was being created in the French region of Bordeaux; over in Napa Valley, the Wappo natives paid no mind to the wild grapevines growing all around them. In Florence, Albiera di Geri degli Agli had a son, Giovanni da Pietro Antinori. Giovanni was the grandson of Vanni di Filippo Antinori, the first businessman in the family. Giovanni was a soldier and diplomat, and his brother, Lodovico, was in the family silk business. They were looking to expand. "Why don't you join the vintners' guild?" their mother reportedly asked them. That was the beginning. They joined the Florentine guild—one of the many such "trade associations" so important to business and art in the city from the twelfth to the sixteenth centuries. The group's coat of arms was a goblet on a white background that can still be seen on a wall on the ground floor of Palazzo Antinori. At the time, "vintners" were wine sellers, but they soon morphed into winemakers as well. We still like to use the word "vintner" (the old Tuscan *vinattiere*)—spoken with a small dose of self-deprecating humor—to describe what we do. To us, it indicates someone who lives for all things wine related.

So maybe I had a little premonition of what was to come when, in 1966, five hundred eighty-one years later, I named my firstborn child Albiera. It was an old family name for the first little leaf on the twenty-sixth branch of the Antinori family tree. Choosing that unusual moniker so many centuries later—and then naming all my daughters with names that begin with A, just like their last name—seemed to give destiny a little push in the right direction. I was following in the footsteps of my own father, who had named his two sons after the founders of the company. In the mid-1800s, the earlier brothers Piero and Lodovico registered their wine cellars with the Ordine degli Imprenditori Vitivinicoli, and in 1895, with their stepbrother, Guglielmo Guerrini, they formed the company Cantine dei Marchesi Piero e Lodovico Antinori. My father wrote that he named my brother and me after the first Piero and Lodovico because he saw a promising future for his successors and his wine, though he did also write that back then "the company did not have vineyards nor even farmland."

In the 1980s, before I saw the light, I assumed that since I had three daughters and my siblings were no longer part of the company, the Antinori family and the company bearing its name would cease to be affiliated with each other. I thought that a dynasty that had lasted for centuries, withstanding bad economic times and political upsets, intrigue at court and parasites on the vines, would simply end after six hundred years. I thought that our family tree, depicted in a painting on the second floor of Palazzo Antinori, which serves as a daily reminder of who we are and where we come from, would wither and die. That tree had become a forest over half a millennium. But I assumed there wouldn't be another generation of Antinoris tending vines and making wines. End of story.

That's why for the first time in twenty-six generations of Antinoris, in 1984 I decided to take on a partner from outside the family. Antinori wines would no longer be ours alone.

I lost a lot of sleep over the decision, and finally I chose an English group that already represented us in the United States and England: Whitbread.

Whitbread was a corporation involved with beer, hotels, and restaurants, founded by Samuel Whitbread in 1742 (a young whippersnapper compared to us!). It started with beer and liquor but had been angling to get more involved with wine for a while. At the time, I saw partnering with Whitbread as a way to keep our company in business and get it back on solid ground financially. We reached an agreement. Tuscan newspaper headlines screamed that foreigners were invading. The generations of Antinoris painted on the walls of Palazzo Antinori in armor, wigs, Renaissance frock coats, and tights looked on in horror as their great-great-great-grandson broke up the family legacy. They would never have dreamed of doing such a thing. For centuries they had included in their wills a *fedecommesso,* an ironclad provision that made all property indivisible, so that it had to be passed down to male heirs, along with the family name.

Our partnership with Whitbread lasted eight long years. During that time, as I'll discuss later in greater detail, two completely opposing viewpoints—regarding everything from what a winemaker is, to what a profit is, to what time is—suffered irreconcilable conflict, to our mutual frustration. It soon became clear that neither I nor the people running Whitbread were happy with the situation. I've seen a lot of large groups enter the wine business and beat a hasty retreat. Whitbread did the same. When it was finished with us, it was finished with vineyards and grapes and all the rest of it.

In 1985, only one year after joining forces with Whitbread, I had my first inkling of how mistaken I'd been in my vision of the future. That was an excellent year for Tuscan reds. At the time I was president of Federvini, the national association of winemakers (formally the Federazione Italiana Industriali Produttori Esportatori e Importatori di Vini, Acquaviti, Liquori, Sciroppi, Aceti e Affini). I was planning to make a promotional trip to the United States and Canada with other representatives of traditional Italian wine families. Albiera was set to come with me; she was nineteen at the time and had just graduated from high school in Florence. She had little experience with wine. I recall a dinner in Florence early that summer, a few months before we were scheduled to go. It was very hot, and she seemed at loose ends. "You don't know what to do with your life," I told her. "Why don't you go and join the harvest in Castello? You could follow the fermentation of the Cervaro and the barrels. You'll get a feel for the environment, see if you like it."

I was talking about our Umbrian vineyard in Castello della Sala, our headquarters for white wines. The fermentation (the moment when the grapes have been harvested and pressed and are left in vats for their sugars to transform into alcohol) I was talking about was the specific fermentation process for Cervaro della Sala, a very unusual white that was just finishing its long and complex gestation. The cold maceration technique we use is unusual for Italian whites and was crucial to the creation of this new wine. Another interesting aspect was the time spent in barriques, the 225- to 230-liter oak casks that we believed indispensable to creating a high-quality version of this wine. The enologist and the cellarers at that point must follow the evolution of the wine in each barrel and taste it periodically. At a certain point before the wine is bottled, it is transferred to smaller barrels, so that the solid residue can be removed and the Cervaro will be "pure" when it is bottled. Basically, I was suggesting that my daughter be abruptly plunged into the Antinori wine laboratory, in the inner sanctum of my enologists. Albiera was surprised and flattered. Most important, she was game. She joined the harvest. She got a feel for the environment. She started to consider a life in wine.

Our trip to the Untied States in spring of 1986 was a present to Albiera for her high school graduation. Neither she nor I really thought of it as an educational wine tour for her; she was just going to stand on the sidelines and watch with pride as I did my work. But then the methanol scandal erupted in Italy. First it came out that producers in Piedmont had added methanol to their wines. Soon the scandal spread; the entire winemaking system was involved. This was truly a low point in Italy's wine history. It caused us to retool all our production, control, and certification methods.

As the president of Federvini, I had to rush back to Italy to calm the waters. But someone had to represent Antinori on the rest of the tour, so I reluctantly left my oldest daughter behind. She had big shoes to fill, and the situation was even more difficult given what was going on back in Italy.

She went from behind-the-scenes observer to a starring role. It turned out to be a wonderful opportunity for her to grow, thanks in part to two pieces of great luck. One was that, in front of an audience of journalists and American wine enthusiasts, she was called upon to talk about Tignanello ("One of the few wines I knew anything about," she admitted later). The other was that my more experienced winemaker friends took her under their wings. When she was on stage and an audience member started to talk trash about Italians and claim that our wine was filled with methanol, half of the delegation would rise up—with Italo Folonari of Ruffino in the lead—to defend the youngest member of the team. She learned what it meant to be part of the larger Italian wine family.

In September, Albiera came back for the Guado al Tasso harvest, and with that she'd experienced a full winemaking cycle: harvest, working in the cellars, and then a new harvest. She learned the rhythm of winemaking, centuries-old processes, and new techniques that we were testing. She learned that wine is a living thing, and that there's nothing repetitive about the cycle required to craft it; it's new each time. A vineyard grows, becomes young, adult, mature, old—and no two vintages are exactly the same. Later in an interview, looking back at that time, she mentioned that that was when she first realized what went into those bottles that were so frequently examined, studied, and discussed by the adult men in Palazzo Antinori. "I was hooked," she said. Quite simply, we had captured her and would never let her go.

And to my great surprise, it turned out that the company's future was already there inside Palazzo Antinori. Anyone who's passionate about wine can learn what she needs to know. An Antinori woman could love this work the same way I did and have the same feeling of belonging to the land and the history. Actually, not just one Antinori woman, but three. Albiera set off a chain reaction, and although her sisters have followed different paths, all those paths have led to our wineries.

Allegra, who went to school in Switzerland, worked first in the wine cellars in Napa Valley that belonged to our friends the Mondavi family. Alessia, "the baby," attended the American School in Florence and then went to college in Milan. She got her degree in agriculture with a specialization in winemaking and enology—and she was one of only two young women in the program. Initially, she planned to study art history. I suggested she try studying wine and see if she liked it, and once she'd made up her mind, she threw herself into it wholeheartedly. I have good instincts about people. I own many vineyards in many places around the world, and I can't possibly be everywhere at once, so being able to read people is a big part of my job. People are like vineyards, in that it's important to understand their qualities and potential, but it's also important to sow seeds in the right kind of soil so that they can blossom and grow to the best of their abilities. The only difference is that people require support and trust rather than sun and water and fertilizer.

Just as Alessia was leaving for Milan, Albiera took charge of the acquisition of a new vineyard in Astigiano, outside of Pescara in Abruzzo, for the Prunotto company. Before she signed the contract, she asked me, "Don't you want to come see it first?"

I answered, "I'm sure you've taken care of everything."

Each of my daughters has had a baptism by fire in front of a large, wine-savvy crowd. For Albiera, it was that experience in the United States. She learned, among other things, that a winemaker has to choose her words carefully, both in the cellars and in front of a microphone. It was a big step toward understanding that the various worlds that form our profession are interconnected. Production and promotion/sales are all part of the job. I think of Alessia as having made her debut then, when she was fifteen or sixteen years old, but she remembers an event several years later as the moment she began to work for the family business. I'd taken her to Chicago with me for a charity auction. We were in that city's beautiful Art Déco-style Opera House.

That evening I spoke a little bit about Italian wine in general before an audience of about five hundred people. As I stepped off the stage, I whispered to her, "In five minutes you have to go up and present our wines." Obviously, poor twenty-two-year-old Alessia knew nothing about this rite of initiation beforehand. Like all my daughters (we're from the Maremma area, whose residents are famous for being tight-lipped), Alessia doesn't like public speaking much, though all three of my daughters have gotten quite practiced at it by now. Alessia was furious with me in that moment, but she already knew a lot about wine, and she turned in an outstanding performance. Did I know it would turn out that way? I'm not really sure. Once on an Italian television show about women in the wine industry, my daughters said, "At first our father steered us gently toward the wine business, and then, all of a sudden, we were in it up to our necks."

In those moments, it dawned on me that my daughters were descended from generations of Chianti winemakers, just as I was. I saw a new future, one in which my own children would share what my grandfather, my father, and I had built. There was only one problem: I was no longer the company's sole decision-maker. I'd ceded power to Whitbread. I had to get the company back into my own hands. I came up with a plan.

"Don't even think about it, Piero. It's nuts!" Vincenzo Maranghi objected when I first shared my plan with him. Maranghi was the Florentine CEO of Mediobanca, protégé and right arm to Enrico Cuccia (the most influential and powerful Italian banker of the contemporary era). At the time, Maranghi was known for having allowed himself all of one week of vacation in his entire working life—and that was back in 1985. He had a long and illustrious career as the top man at one of the biggest banks in the country and in all of Europe. Maranghi lived for his work. He'd seen it all and done it all. But when, in 1992, I asked him for a big loan so that I could buy back the stake in the company that I'd sold to the British, he was shocked. Why would I want to do that? Whitbread was a major business group. Listed on the stock exchange. Solid. It had helped me out of a tough situation. Most of all, this was a bad time to take out a loan.

Antinori had grown a lot during that time. It had earned an international reputation, and Whitbread wouldn't willingly give up its investment. In fact, Maranghi told me, Whitbread wanted to do the opposite. Rumor in the financial world was that this giant English corporation was trying to acquire a majority stake in Antinori. Then it planned to use my not-enormous-but-prestigious company as the main draw when it tried to sell its liquor business for a profit to Allied Lyons (Allied Domecq at the time), an ambitious liquor corporation that was trying to get into the wine field. My partners had a dual goal: maximizing the investment they'd made and simultaneously getting out of a business that had turned out to be difficult and unprofitable.

"This is high finance, Piero," Maranghi told me. "Lyons only wants to buy if it can have a controlling interest in Antinori. If Whitbread doesn't have Antinori, Lyons won't come to the table. Whitbread is going to ask a high price for the shares you want to buy in order to cover the profit it will be missing out on. The figure will be outrageous. It's a huge risk for you, the wineries, and us." We were playing a real-life game of Monopoly, but I was certain about one thing: I only wanted to continue to work as a winemaker—and I really did want to continue to work as a winemaker—if I could retain complete control.

"What would you put up as collateral for the loan?" Maranghi asked.

"My own money, and . . ."

"And what?"

"And Palazzo Antinori."

"The house your family has lived in for centuries. The house your father finally managed to buy back. Are you sure?"

I began telling him what I'd been doing and thinking. I told him about the wines that I—and my increasingly involved daughters—

were making. And the ones we wanted to make. And the new land we were eyeing in Tuscany and in other parts of Italy and around the world. We'd designed new cellars. We'd won awards, and our exports were growing. Gradually, I convinced him that getting Antinori back wasn't simply a sentimental gambit.

It was risky, that's for sure, and we Antinoris don't like risk. For centuries in Florence the name Antinori had been synonymous with cautious behavior, diplomacy, and the very Italian skill of wriggling out of spots between a rock and a hard place—or, more specifically, between potentates and bureaucrats. We have a long collective memory, and I mean really long—centuries long. We were still a little upset by that time in the early 1500s that Alessandro di Niccolò Antinori, a banker, was forced to declare bankruptcy after falling into a financial hole. Like half of Florence, he had drained his coffers to make enormous loans to the European monarchies that were at war with one another—and those loans were never repaid. I was haunted by the fact that in his day, English royalty had been the worst defaulters. Since then, we Antinoris had focused on grapes and trade and politics, but we'd stayed out of the banking business.

When it was time to make the great leap, I once again spent sleepless nights in my room on the third floor of Palazzo Antinori. My father, who had closely followed me and all my projects with a curiosity that belied his age, had passed away in November 1991. He'd been such a big help to me. "If you need advice, I'm here," he'd always say. "Depend on yourself for the rest." I could lean on Albiera, though. My daughter had just turned twenty-five and didn't have an official title at the company yet, but she assisted me and supported me at every turn. And then there was my friend Alessandro Pazzi, a Florentine lawyer. Today he is the only person besides enologist Renzo Cotarella, our CEO, who is not a member of the Antinori family and sits on our board of directors.

I had the element of surprise on my side. Whitbread was going to offer to buy my shares, unaware that I'd been preapproved for the large loan I would need to regain control. I was making a bet, taking a calculated risk. From his little cloud of red wine atop Mount Olympus, the god Bacchus offered me a hand. I'm not talking about a good harvest or inspiration for a new vineyard. Instead, I unexpectedly obtained the economic resources I needed to approach the final showdown with a little more confidence.

For years, I'd held a minority share in Fondiaria Assicurazioni, a financial services company. It so happened that at the time the largest financial groups in the country had set their sights on that historic Florentine company as part of a big play for corporate stakes. Raul Gardini was at peak power. (Gardini was nicknamed "the farmer" and "the pirate of Ravenna" because of his blunt manner and his unorthodox method of navigating the shark-filled waters of Italian finance. In fact, he got caught in the undertow of those waters in the summer of 1993, when he was one of the high-profile suicides during the beginning of Tangentopoli, the corruption scandal that rattled the Italian worlds of politics and business.) Just the year before, this fearless businessman, sniffing out his prey, had set himself the task of vacuuming up any crumb of Fondiaria stock in order to gain a majority stake. Gardini and his group, the Montedison fleet, were flush, and overnight my shares became highly desirable. I immediately sold them and invested the proceeds—a completely unexpected windfall—in the transaction. It was all set.

When a beaming Albiera and I toasted the agreement with glasses of Chianti Classico in London, the representatives of the English company seemed to have a bitter taste in their mouths. Maybe they hadn't thought we could pull it off. They knew, or at least thought they knew, how much money I had. And they approached the whole thing as a financial group, not a winemaking group trying to make arrangements for the next three or four generations.

The company and the brand were ours again. My dream had come true. And time would prove that we'd made the right move. Our wines grew popular all over the world in the next few years, so we could easily cover the Mediobanca loan. Lots of people were shocked. In the first few years of our newfound independence, plenty of people came forward to float potential partnerships or offer to acquire part or all of the company. Maybe they thought that after a gesture that was "more romantic than logical" (that's what my brother, Lodovico, called it in an interview), our coffers were empty and our position precarious. The first thing I did when I returned from London after that triumphal trip in 1992 was to add the phrase "Twenty-Six Generations" to our labels, brochures, letterhead, and all other business documents. Our history, begun so many centuries earlier, was back on track. And we were not only aware of that, but proud of it.

Today, the continuation of that history is widely acknowledged, and our business has gone down in the annals of history. In April 2008, *The Wall Street Journal* published one of the most exhaustive and interesting articles that I've ever read about Marchesi Antinori. Writing from Florence, journalist Gabriel Kahn expressed deep admiration for our "vintage strategy," an ancient approach that still manages to be forward-thinking while requiring long-term thinking and carefully considered methods—so different from the fast-paced rhythm employed in the United States. Our strategy has been around forever, true, but its success makes it current. That's what I'd like people to understand.

A few months later, *60 Minutes* did a long report on us. Morley Safer interviewed me in my office. Then we toured Palazzo Antinori. The piece included interviews with my daughters, who were shown working in our vineyards in Tuscany and California. The program covered our history, from my ancestors joining the vintners' guild to the surprising ascendancy of women in the company in the previous decade. With a typically straightforward American approach, our ups and downs were not presented as "strange but true," or some overnight success, but instead as a case of entrepreneurial excellence. The American audience was introduced to a concept that is near and dear to my heart, which is that keeping our business in the family and working to improve our wines are not sentimental choices or just the traditional way of doing things, but the best and maybe even the only way for us to do our most fruitful work possible over time.

Today we are discussing how to pass on our family name and the marquisate through my daughters. We're looking at the next six centuries. We're looking to my grandchildren. Vittorio, Albiera's son and the oldest in his generation, is eighteen and is studying economics. He's already spent a summer working in the offices of our importers in Great Britain and the United States. Niccolò, Allegra's oldest, is eleven. He played with the bottling machine at our estate in California last summer, just so that he could begin touching and smelling wine. His mother complains that I monopolize his time, but I'm just a good grandfather. Then there are my granddaughters. Albiera's daughter, Verdiana, is sixteen and is already traveling the world. Vivia, ten, is Allegra's youngest and is very promising. Our most recent arrival—at the time of this writing, Giovanni Piero, caused Alessia to stop her constant traveling in late 2010. These kids' mothers and I, their grandfather, don't want them to feel pressured; they have to follow their own paths. We're not trying to make them obsessed with barrels and dynasties. We'd like them to have experiences away from home and outside of Italy with things that don't necessarily have anything to do with wine. Going out into the world has been important for everyone in my family, perhaps for me most of all. But I'd be lying if I denied that we hope eventually wine will call to them.

2

VILLA ANTINORI

Becoming a Winemaker

*V*illa Antinori, a Chianti Classico and one of the most widely known wines in the world, is a full-blooded Tuscan red. Yes, a small amount of international grapes are added to its pure Chianti Sangiovese base. But those grapes are grown in our vineyards and then aged in our cellars. This wine was born about ten years before I was, in 1928. We have the same father—Niccolò Antinori, the man who was so struck by the excellence of the great wines of Bordeaux that he formulated a whole new vision for wine. He wanted to create something that stepped outside of the box and defied the conventions of the time.

The first thing that was innovative about this wine was that it used only grapes that we grew on the estates my father had gradually acquired and upgraded over the years. These days, all fine wines are made this way, with the winemaker controlling the supply chain, but back then it wasn't a given.

He ignored the rules a second time—the experts called him "clever"—and knowingly combined Chianti Classico and French Cabernet grapes. Those Cabernet grapes from Tignanello were the real surprise. Farmers in that area didn't know a lot about those "foreign" grapes, and they had been largely overlooked for half a century. Yet Cabernet was and is (and hopefully will remain into the future) one of Antinori's best grapes.

Then he turned to the packaging. At the time, Chianti was sold in straw-covered flasks with round bottoms. He bottled this new wine in Bordeaux-style wine bottles with wide necks and shoulders. He was aiming to compete with the French wines he'd seen displayed like precious jewels in London shop windows.

Finally, it was time to select a name. "They have châteaux, but we have villas," said the best vintner in our family's twenty-fourth generation of vintners, i.e., my father. He graced his creation with the name of the estate on Strada Pisana where many Antinoris had been born and others were resting for eternity in a chapel dedicated to the Virgin Mary. Even the idea of having the villa depicted on the label was new in Italy. Family legend has it that the artwork was by my great-aunt Ernestina Ludolf, the sister of Nathalie Antinori, my grandfather's wife. Sadly, the villa doesn't belong to the family anymore. It was horribly damaged by Allied bombing, then underwent a different kind of assault from the factories and other large industrial buildings that sprang up in the area in the 1960s. (At one time, the villa enjoyed a clear view of the domes and bell towers of Florence.) Also, it's located outside the official Chianti Classico geographic area. A family from Prato now owns it.

Villa Antinori wine, however, still exists. It's a traditional but refined red that continues to earn praise. Indeed, it's now one of our best-known wines, and is fully mature after steady improvements. Since 2001 it's been elevated to an IGT (Indicazione Geografica Tipica) Toscana wine, though it's kept its essence and we haven't changed even a single comma on the label.

For me, this wine is all about memories and tradition. It links today's Marchesi Antinori to the many centuries when my ancestors produced and sold flasks in Italy and abroad. It's the basis, too, for a number of wines that my family created afterward that went on to make history in Chianti. A bottle of Villa Antinori contains not only wine, but a whole history of wine.

Just as Tignanello would in the 1970s, Villa Antinori invigorated our business at a time when all seemed lost. My father wrote of those early years, "The family wine business had a fragile foundation and an uncertain future." It's true that our family was well-known in Italy for wine. And in 1873, the Marchese Niccolò, my father's grandfather, had earned a certificate of honor at the World's Fair for his work as a small producer and seller of wine. But there was nothing that would have led anyone to believe that there were large-scale wineries in our future.

Guglielmo Guerrini, our rather surly ancestor, handled bureaucratic and administrative procedures for the company formed in 1895. According to my father, he was both the first to lay the foundation for the modern company and the person who brought progress to a halt for a long time. Descended from an old Roman banking family, he had a closed mind and was against reform. His idea of a company meeting was to assemble others before him and begin giving orders and strict instructions to his children and grandchildren, many of whom began to hate the brand and the wine and left to pursue other interests. To make things even worse, his stepbrothers

Lodovico and Piero soon divvied up the business. One wanted the land and the fields, and the other wanted the cellars and the wine-making facilities. Before my father would have a chance to "give in" and accept winemaking as his destiny, and before he could get the older generation to let him take over the cellars, he would serve as a soldier in the trenches in World War I, and then as a salesman who traveled all over the world. He often doubted that he would ever be able to make a life in wine for himself. But eventually it came to pass.

These days, the concept of the family business is much discussed. It's been well established that this kind of enterprise is fragile. According to two studies from the late 1990s, one Swiss and one English, 40 percent of family businesses decline and then disappear the first time they pass from one generation to the next. Only 15 percent survive past the second generation. That's usually because there's no obvious leader among the natural-born heirs—no one with the passion, background, charisma, and dedication to take the reins. Or because simply handing down the business automatically generates stagnation. Later generations just hang on to the family name and don't innovate or grow; they stay the same over time, overshadowed by a patriarch who keeps postponing his own retirement. Not to mention the internal rivalries, usually between members of the same generation. My father dealt with these issues, and so did I.

However, it should also be noted that the family business formula has stood the test of time. It has produced rewarding results and great progress in various eras and social contexts, from Manhattan to emerging markets. In recent years, family business theory has become a hot topic among economists. Today, they say that keeping know-how and decision-making power in the hands of a limited group united by personal—not just economic—interests that are renewed with each generation tends to result in a system of very cohesive knowledge, experience, and practices. That kind of energy, nourished by passion and tradition and refined over time, probably cannot be created using some management formula. But you need a strong foundation. John Davis at Harvard Business School, who specializes in the study of what makes a family business long lasting, has noted, "By the end of every generation, family firms need to have built a reservoir of trust, pride, and money so that the next generation has enough of them to maintain the momentum of the business and the spirit of the family."

But that's all theory. I'm the twenty-fifth descendant to lead a family brand that persists eight hundred thirty-two years after the date of the first official document bearing the Antinori name, a parchment that records legal transfer of ownership between Accarisio Antinori of Combiate and the San Michele Arcangelo monastery in Passignano. I'm still building wineries six hundred twenty-six years after my family joined the winemakers' trade association.

In 2008, the magazine *Family Business* published a list of the world's oldest family businesses. We were number ten. First on the list was a Japanese family that has built Buddhist temples for 1,429 years and whose 40 generations are listed on a ceremonial scroll 3 meters long. My daughters and I have all asked ourselves, "How?" How is it that despite war, political revolt, and financial disaster, not to mention family infighting and conflicting personalities and ideas, for 7 centuries Antinoris have kept the business going without breaking the chain?

Our country is definitely part of the answer to that riddle. With all the many different nations and civilizations in the world, an astonishing five Italian companies made that list of long-lived family businesses. Those companies have histories that predate the existence of Italy itself anywhere but in the minds of Dante and a few other enlightened people. Then there is the importance of family, tradition, and respect for elders in Italian culture. And there's something else many of us on that list have in common. Out of all the possible businesses, three families in the top ten have worked in the same field for centuries—wine: the French de Goulaine family, our neighbors the Ricasoli family (who took back their company in the 1990s), and us. There are plenty of other long-standing wine families that didn't make this particular list, such as the Frescobaldi and Mazzei families, whose ancestor Filippo Mazzei helped Thomas Jefferson plant a vineyard in Virginia.

Is wine the secret to longevity, binding men and women who lived three, four, and five hundred years ago to us with a long thread? Antinoris have been silk and wool merchants, bankers, diplomats, artists, scholars, and warriors. But wine has always been a part of our family's history. It became one of the family's main businesses in the mid-sixteenth century. Consider that Alessandro di Niccolò, the financier, lent money to the kings of France and sold wheat and silk, but he also requested Grand Duke Cosimo de' Medici's help with a shipment of Malvasia seized in Messina due to war. Or look at Filippo Antinori, who tried to get into the retail wine market in the Papal States. As far back as the eighteenth and nineteenth centuries, Antinoris fended off the wine aphids and began to produce the best wines in Tuscany, celebrated by poets and courtiers.

Allow me to reflect on my own history, too. Wine runs through every part of my life like a red river, linking who I was as a child to my current identity. I tasted wine for the first time when I was five or six, some nameless Chianti. On holidays, kids got wine diluted with a little water. Every Tuscan child was initiated this way. The favorite dessert of every child in our region was and still is bread sprinkled with red wine and sugar. From a very early age—for as long as I can remember—wine has been associated with pleasure for me.

I recall the smell of our red grapes from an even earlier time— Sangiovese grapes so dark they were almost black, growing close together and hanging heavy on the vine. Grapes that soon were going to produce great Tuscan reds. Grapes cultivated, beloved, and celebrated by the Romans and before them by the Etruscans. Grapes descended from the divine. The ancient name of these grapes isn't from some Catholic saint. It comes from the Latin *sanguis Jovis,* Jupiter's blood. In October, the countryside was heavily perfumed with their scent. It hung over the vineyards, the fields, and the hills where I went hunting with my father. (He loved to go hunting with his dogs. He'd leave at dawn with some friends and a big basket of food and drink.) Early in the month, everyone in my family would ritually stop as we passed through the vineyards to pluck some sweet, ripe grapes from the vine and eat them.

Then, one fateful morning in late July 1944, when I had just turned six, my father and I rode our bicycles from Montefiridolfi to the Santa Cristina Chianti estate in Tignanello, north of Siena.

There, my father received an alarming phone call from San Casciano Val di Pesa, further north near Florence. We'd had wine cellars there since 1898. Piero and Lodovico Antinori had intended that site to be the center of the modern company and house all the family business related to wine, which had grown scattered and disorganized over time. For years, my grandfather and my father had been experimenting with winemaking and aging techniques in the cool darkness of those cellars. Now my father and I rounded up an old wagon and a pair of horses and rushed to the scene. A full kilometer away, the air was thick with the smell of wine and grape must.

In those days, Italy was feeling the effects of the last difficult gasps of the war. The Allied forces had entered San Casciano after cannon fire and two rounds of bombing, and the Germans were retreating in chaos. Those were terrible times for Tuscany. The Chianti area had been devastated. Many buildings had been demolished with explosives; mines and wreckage filled the countryside. I remember that when the storm finally passed, someone calculated that more than half the buildings in the municipal records had been destroyed or damaged, either by Allied bombs or by the defeated Germans, who caused havoc as they were chased out. Houses were lost, but also bell towers, churches, castles, buildings that had been there since the Middle Ages. Our family villa was also hit, because it stood near an electric plant, making it a military target.

The Germans had tromped through the San Casciano winery—the people who live there to this day just call it "the cellars"—looking for men and provisions. Instead, they found barrels of Chianti Classico and bottles stacked along the walls to age. Naturally, the wine was defenseless. Wine knows nothing of war and armistice. The Germans didn't have time to drink the wine they found, and they had no way to bring it back to Germany, so they simply raised their machine guns and shot the barrels and bottles. They systematically destroyed the wine so that the enemy couldn't enjoy it either. My father noted this senseless violence in his records, writing, "One building fallen, roofs torn off, machinery disassembled . . ." And most of all, rivulets of red wine dripping everywhere. Soaking into the ground. Lost and wasted. Ruined.

That scent of young Chianti saturated everything. It was the smell of destruction, years of work and commitment obliterated for no reason, and for me it is an indelible memory. In the moment, I knew that something was very wrong and would have to be set right. I exchanged a look with my father, who had really wanted me to be there. His eyes said, one day, there will be good wine in these cellars again. Better wine even. Wine, I understood in that moment, is the fruit of hope, planning, and responsibility.

Gradually, I entered the world of wine and learned its secrets. A world of beauty and work, but also fun, where my path from employee to future head of the company proceeded smoothly. At fifteen, I began to study and taste wine seriously, first Italian wines and then wines from all over the world. That was also when I began to follow the various stages of the harvest and winemaking on our estates and in the cellars. I could recall many extraordinary harvest seasons in Chianti. In particular, the season before the war stood out, and still does to this day. That was when for the first time I learned to love the unique smell of grape must fermenting in the vats, the scent of that mysterious process during which the smell of must evolves into the intense and fragrant aroma of wine.

In later years, when the company was recovering and the cellars—which, after the war, had even housed the Jeeps of Canadian soldiers—were once again filled with intact bottles, I studied at the classical high school in Florence and then at the university. I planned to study agriculture, but my father advised me to take classes in economics and business instead. ("There are plenty of good technicians out there, but businesses around here fail because they don't know how to balance their books!") Fortunately, professor Roberto Bracco—a prophet of economics, a brilliant Florentine who had been head of the local chamber of commerce and the Bank of Tuscany—took me under his wing and suggested that I write my thesis on the business of agriculture. For four years I studied, attended classes, and took exams, but I was never terribly enthusiastic. I don't think I even collected my diploma. The experience was useful training, but I already understood that my destiny lay elsewhere. I wanted to be tested a different way.

During my time as a student, I hung around the company offices more and more. As a student apprentice, I did a little of everything, and I often was responsible for writing correspondence. Computers were unheard of back then. We were still tap-tapping on typewriters and cranking out carbon copies. Those company missives employed a stiff, ceremonious language, phrases that I used myself for years without even knowing what they meant. But as soon as I had a chance, I ducked out from behind my desk and wandered around the sales area, where there were letters coming in from all over the world and packing slips for grapes and wines that were arriving and departing.

I don't remember feeling anxious about my growing responsibilities, and I believe my daughters would say the same. Even being the oldest didn't put undue pressure on me. Maybe that's because I always had an excellent relationship with my father. And he always believed in me. Or maybe because even before I truly understood the work we do, I already saw it as more a privilege than a duty.

After forty-five years behind the big desk in Palazzo Antinori, I can't imagine that any other profession would give me so much pleasure and reward me so greatly. Antinoris have always treated wine with respect, and wine has given us happy and intense lives.

A life in high-level viticulture has everything: tradition, direct contact with land and nature, the art of hospitality, and the little pleasures of daily life. There are opportunities to mingle with an international community that is full of interesting, pleasant, and creative people. There is travel, a chance to see beautiful places on five continents, because grapes always seem to grow best in gorgeous surroundings. I love traveling. About fifteen years ago, the market began to expand, and we increased our partnerships, consulting relationships, and collaborations, as well as acquired land abroad to start up production of our wine in various places. There are frequent trips to far-flung spots that I now consider home. Two or three times a year at least I visit our vineyards in the United States. At least once a year I go to Asia to investigate newly emerging markets. I never miss a big wine event. But there are also more exploratory journeys made in search of good land and good ideas. Often on those I've been accompanied by my enologist, first Giacomo Tachis (the "Father of Italian Wine") and later Renzo Cotarella. Traveling opens your mind. Through travel, I went from being an Antinori apprentice to a part of the company in my own right.

After a long apprenticeship as an "inspector" (today that would be someone responsible for covering a certain area) for the company in Italy, first in Lazio and Campania and then in Lombardy, in the early 1960s I planned a grand tour of our importers in New York. At the last minute, my father asked me to pass through Toronto first to meet our new importer for Canada, who'd been hired by letter without any of us ever laying eyes on him. Maybe my father wanted to see whether (and how) I would be capable of evaluating the people who worked for us, especially those responsible for representing us around the world.

Upon arriving in Canada, I was introduced to a chatty Polish man named something like Simonovic. He immediately informed me that he represented a lot of the era's big-name Italian companies in Canada. His clients included Cavallino Rosso, a brandy that was very trendy at the time and advertised on the seminal Italian television program, *Carosello*. In other words, he had impressive credentials. We talked for a while, and then he suggested that I stay in Canada longer than planned so that I could visit the major liquor monopolies (in Canada, alcoholic beverages are all under state control) in the various provinces.

I accepted, mostly because I wanted to learn as much as possible about that complex market. But there was one problem: the dollars to be used for my trip had been wired to New York, where they were waiting for me. My Canadian detour had only been planned at the last minute and was supposed to be a quick visit. I didn't have the cash for my first major business trip on foreign soil. I called my father. He quickly responded, "Ask our guy to advance you the money."

"No problem," Simonovic replied when I did. "We'll settle up later." The arrangement sounded fine at the time, but after a couple of days, I started to worry. My host was a big spender, and he had fancy taste: luxury hotels, caviar, Champagne. It was a little much for a young man on the first business trip of his career. I had nothing against his choices, but I immediately began to grow concerned about that final bill. We were a medium-small business at the time; my father would have gasped if he had seen some of the numbers we were racking up. To boot, I wasn't so sure about my companion's wine knowledge, judging by the visits we made to the directors of the various monopolies as we traveled from city to city.

Montreal, Calgary, Winnipeg, Regina, the capital of Saskatchewan. It was an exotic trip to places where Italian wine—and wine in general—was still fairly unknown. Then as now, anyone who wanted to sell wine in Canada had to be approved and placed on a special list recorded in each office in every province capital. At the end of our time crisscrossing Canada, we met the director of the liquor board for Victoria. He was an old, retired English officer, Colonel McCougan. He'd ended up behind a desk after an adventuresome life that spanned the commonwealth. A life whose bright spots were largely supplied by whiskey and gin, I imagine, because after I'd spent an hour trying to pique his interest in our wine, he turned a skeptical eye to me and said, "There's no future for wine in Canada, kid." I like to think of that moment now, after 2010, when for the first time Italy topped France in the number of wines exported to Canada.

Finally, it was time to settle the bill with the good-natured Simonovic before I left for New York. I practiced the nonchalant expression I would wear when I saw that astronomical bill, and then in the morning I waited for him in the hotel restaurant. But he didn't show. There was a surprise twist: it turned out he'd checked out an hour earlier with all his bags. His hotel bill was paid up. He'd been in a big hurry. Shocked by this strange situation and a little upset that I would have this bill hanging over my head, I did the only thing I could do and flew to Manhattan to start my apprenticeship. I was confident that sooner or later Simonovic would come looking for his money. But I was wrong. I didn't hear from him during the rest of my sojourn in North America.

When my time in the United States was finished, I returned to Italy and immediately wrote to our importer to get the damn bill. And then I waited for an answer. For months I asked daily whether there was any mail for me, and there never was. I didn't feel right about owing money to someone who worked for us in a foreign country. Enterprising Vanni di Filippo Antinori, the manager of the company in the early Middle Ages, would never have done that. Nor would Alessandro di Niccolò, who in the sixteenth century already had a sales office in Toledo and sold casks in Djerba and Algiers. It nagged at me. I decided to write directly to the Italian Embassy in Canada, asking for a new address or any other recent news of the whereabouts of the Polish man who claimed to represent so many major Italian companies there. Surely they'd know him. At first the embassy wouldn't give me a straight answer. They hemmed and hawed. They stonewalled. Then, finally, they admitted to knowing the man I was describing and made an astonishing confession: the person I sought, who had always seemed slightly off to me, had vanished into thin air. He'd probably disappeared behind the Iron Curtain. The Iron Curtain? Yes, because they were pretty sure that Simonovic was actually an undercover KGB agent who'd fled Canada because he'd been recognized and pursued. A hedonistic Russian spy with a passion for enology and an excellent command of Italian. I didn't try to pay my debt after that. Who would I have paid? It was a unique experience, to say the least, to live high on the hog, staying in expensive hotels and eating and drinking fine food and wine, all on the tab of the Soviet secret service!

A few years later, I took a long trip to Sweden and Finland, where liquor is also controlled by monopolies and companies need to be registered to sell it. Our agent there was a large man and a big drinker. The local alcoholic beverages wreaked havoc on my stomach. Then I stopped in England, Germany, and Belgium. Germans weren't terribly fond of Italian wine at the time. The only wines that really sold there were big bottles with screw tops rather than corks that were bought almost exclusively by Italians who had emigrated to Germany. They drank to forget their days laboring in factories and mines and to fuel their nostalgia. Educated drinkers had a negative impression of Italian wine, especially as compared to the wine from Bordeaux, which was closer geographically. We had been trying to break into the market for some time, but with poor results. We needed a platform, a credible sponsor, someone who would recognize the progress we'd made with our wines over the previous half century.

I looked for an expert and well-known agent experienced with high-quality wines (all of them French at the time). I found the ideal person and company—very well-known and very influential, perfect for creating a new image for our wines. The problem was that when I wrote to Michael Bömers, head of Reidemeister & Ulrich, the biggest wine import and distribution firm in Germany at the time, he immediately responded that he wasn't interested in Italian wines and didn't think they were good enough for his brand. I pushed to meet with him in person, and that's how I ended up in Bremen in the middle of "hostile territory." This was the port where the untouchable French *Grands Crus* had long been unloaded from the barges that sailed down the Weser River and then were distributed and ended up on the tables and in the wine cellars of Germans with refined taste.

The night before, in London, during my short trip to England, I had hosted a charity dinner. At the time, England was much more enthusiastic about Italian wines. It had been one of the first foreign countries to appreciate what was going on in our wineries. I sat at a table with my importers, and I was offered a selection of really high-quality wines. They were all excellent, and yet again, many of them were French. One bottle, however, was truly special. When I drank it, a wave of pleasure washed over me. I knew I was experiencing perfection. I'm talking about one of the best wines I've ever tasted, an experience so intense that the label is imprinted on my mind. I can see it perfectly even forty years later. It was a 1959 Chateau La Mission Haut-Brion. A Graves. That was a vintage whose quality is still discussed in reverential terms today.

Bremen. My German hosts courteously informed me that we'd talk business over breakfast. We met in their office. A line of reds sat on the desk, three or four of them in carafes, no labels or other indications of what they were. Was this some local tradition? I doubted that these were wines from a tap at some bar. Were the Germans going to test me before they would agree to work with us? Were they trying to determine whether we barbarian Chianti vintners really knew about wine?

The first was a red Tuscan Chianti Classico. Actually, it was ours, my father's great reborn Chianti. A 1967 Villa Antinori. It was especially recognizable to me because that had been my first harvest; I'd taken over the company the previous year. It was the wine that baptized me as a vintner, and it and I had been blessed with an extraordinary autumn for Sangiovese. I found it comforting to meet up with it there, in the middle of beer-drinking country. I knew it immediately, of course. Did they think I would have trouble identifying the red I'd grown up drinking? They began to look at me differently, I could tell.

"Try this one." If this was a test, I was passing with flying colors. The second wine was more difficult, however. I hesitated. My proctors watched me closely. Michael Bömers, an expert who would go on to work with us for a long time, and his purchasing director were probably smug in the belief that the trap they'd set had caught the young and inexperienced Mediterranean winemaker who stood before them. "We went easy with the first one, but now we'll see how he does," I imagined them thinking. I tasted it. I concentrated.

"It's a Bordeaux."

"Okay," they said, "but there are a lot of Bordeaux wines."

"Left bank," I ventured. And at the same time a light bulb was coming on for me. Yes! It was the same wine that I'd enjoyed so much a few hours earlier in London. Or at least I was pretty sure it was.

"The left bank is long," they said.

"Perhaps from Graves."

"Excellent!"

When they reacted that way, I knew I had it right. I played it up a little, swirling the red liquid in the glass and holding it up to the light to study it.

"Mission Haut-Brion!"

They were speechless. Then they recovered and asked, "And the year?"

"1959!"

That afternoon they signed a contract with us. I'm sure that morning they weren't planning on signing. Bacchus had smiled upon the Antinoris yet again.

A half century later, the Germans are among our biggest importers. As for the myth of the unbeatable French, in June 2011 it was announced that in 2010, Italy, which had been a secondary wine supplier among the elite since the 1960s, outstripped the French in wine production. Yes, according to the European Commission, we are the number one wine producer worldwide: 49,600,000 hectoliters as compared to 46,200,000 from our competitors. By 2002 we had already taken over the largest wine market outside of Europe, the United States, where our exports have continued to grow. To those who would caution not to confuse quantity with quality, I'd note that we have also beaten the Bordeaux masters in the number of DOC, IGT, and DOCG certifications earned. All at a time when many are reducing production because they can't expand their markets.

Back in Florence in the mid-1960s, it was time for me to take my place among the company's executives. My father and I planned to do this gradually over four to five years. First I was going to have to take a long break from vats and accounting records. After a lot of effort—seemingly infinite papers to be filled out and documents to be submitted—I was about to have a long-nurtured dream come true. I was going to serve in the aeronautic branch of Italy's military with a group of old friends from Florence.

Military service has been an important part of my family's history. Our much-discussed and apparently moody and difficult relative, Giovan Francesco, aka Morticino, is reported to have been a very skilled mercenary who distinguished himself defending Florence against a siege by Holy Roman Emperor Charles V in 1530. My great-grandfather Niccolò was a hero who fought the Austrians in 1848, in the Battle of Curtatone and Montanara during the First Italian War of Independence. My father served voluntarily in World War I, where he was part of the Battle of Caporetto and the Italian retreat and, as a liaison officer, the Battle of Piave, until he entered Trieste in late October 1918, when the city had finally become Italian. I wanted to experience the military and I'd worked hard to get there.

But then there was one of those events that sometimes occur and change a person's life. They often take the form of challenges—things need to be figured out and decisions need to be made. At that time, Vincenzo Benazzi was my father's right-hand man. From Romagna, he was an unstoppable worker and had a lifetime's worth of experience with wine on tap and table wine, and he'd traveled throughout Italy selling them. I don't recall exactly how he came to work for Antinori, but he distinguished himself with his initiative and knowledge of the field. He was a true self-made man. He made the company run smoothly from behind a big desk in a room at the end of the courtyard in our Florentine headquarters. There was a smaller desk next to his, and that was where I sat while I assisted him and sometimes studied. The more I studied, though, the more I knew I wanted something other than the life of a scholar.

I knew high-quality wine was the way to go. We needed bottles people would choose and keep and remember. My boss, Benazzi, came from another planet as far as wine was concerned. A place where the culture of wine was a luxury for a small niche. He was all about the mass market, where the best winery was the one that produced the most in the least amount of time and with the smallest investment. The scent of that low-quality wine seemed to waft in and out of our office. For centuries that type of wine had been fuel for people working in the fields, medicine that was used to treat all ills, and a companion who made the evening more bearable. Passion, though, had nothing to do with it. I dreamed of a perfect wine that I would see ripen slowly and artfully in our cellars. I had different ideas, but there was a hierarchy in place and a schedule to follow. Benazzi kept a tight rein on his contact list and the part of the business that was still mysterious to me and had to do with bureaucracy and accounting records. I felt I had talent for that work, but I probably needed to develop and mature.

Our agent in central Italy was the first to raise the alarm: someone had gotten sick after drinking our wine. Was that even possible? We investigated. Just a little nausea, it turned out. No one could prove it was due to our wine. We brushed it off, and then we forgot about it completely. But then more reports came in from all over Italy. Finally, there was one we could not ignore: Benazzi himself, the company's CEO, had gotten sick after taking his usual lunch break with a sandwich and a glass of wine (ours, of course).

An internal investigation was launched, and the guilty party was soon identified in a half-empty bag in one of the cellars. At the time, there were no "organic" standards; rules for production were vague. Today, an enologist is an expert in yeasts and bacteria, but at the time an enologist was a combination chemist and sorcerer's apprentice whose main job was to decide how to prepare wines for exportation and storage at the end of an industrial winemaking process that was pretty seat-of-the-pants and imprecise. Potassium tartrate was used for this purpose. Later, too late, we'd learn that this substance had a twin that looked identical to it but was a powerful emetic. Our supplier, a famous company in Milan that shall remain nameless, had mixed up the two in a shipment.

Panic ensued. Products weren't easily traced at the time. Which Chiantis were making people sick? Where had they been sold? We suspended all activity and for a couple of months our entire staff traveled around the country tasting bottles, with orders to recall any that might even possibly have been contaminated. In the anxious weeks that followed, thousands of innocent bottles may have been destroyed for no reason. Our relationships with many excellent distributors were compromised. The news got out. After a few weeks, the Antinori brand was on very shaky ground. We needed to do something. Benazzi was close to retirement. It seemed to have been his mistake. In any case, he generously and nobly accepted all responsibility. My father compensated him, and he retired.

The tartrate crisis seemed to be resolved, but my father had a new problem: he needed a replacement for the sixty-eight-year-old Benazzi. I was twenty-eight and about to leave for my military service. My father said, "It's your turn. From now on, we have to be the face of Antinori."

In a few days, he managed to find a legal loophole that said that as the oldest child of an elderly parent, I was exempt from military service. I wasn't happy about it, but that's how it went. Instead of slowly integrating myself into the company, I took a flying leap from low-level employee to executive and public face of the family. Rather than my father solemnly passing me the reins, I had a baptism by fire. My father had been chomping at the bit to take over the company when it was his turn, and then he wanted to burnish its image. I, however, may have been put in charge too early. It was 1966. Italy was experiencing an economic boom. Burgundy was having an excellent year and making some of its best white wines ever.

That year ended with the terrible flood in Florence. In November, six meters of water filled the historic center of the city. There were dozens of victims, and the art in the Uffizi was submerged in fuel oil. Water rushed into the cellar of our palazzo, destroying many of the old bottles stored there. But if those were tragic days, they were also days when the world showed an outpouring of love for our city. Thousands of young people from all over Europe came to shovel mud and bring books and paintings into the sun where they could dry. It was in many ways the start of a new era for Tuscany. As the twenty-fifth head of the Antinori family, I was poised to be part of it.

3

SOLAIA

Growing a Style

*S*omeone who decides to celebrate a truly special occasion by opening a bottle of Solaia from 1986—or 1982, or even 1979 (I turned forty that year, my daughter Alessia, four) is rewarded with a wine that is not only "welcoming" and well developed, but maintains all the freshness and fruity background that it had when we put it in the cellar to age. This wine is elegant, rather than powerful, the perfect expression of an international grape—Cabernet—that has learned to do things the Tuscan way, as our enologist Giacomo Tachis so beautifully put it.

In many ways, Solaia is the wine of my dreams. Like the best French wines, it has a flavor that improves over the years, and an unmistakable personality. Drinking it is a pleasure, but also an intellectual exercise: it's a wine for true wine lovers. Its significance needs to be teased out and parsed a little. If Villa Antinori and Chianti Classico Badia a Passignano are Renaissance frescoes, Solaia is a work of contemporary art—conceptual. It plays off a classic foundation in surprising ways.

The Solaia vineyard is located next to the Tignanello vineyard, in the sunniest corner of our old Santa Cristina estate, in Mercatale Val di Pesa, south of Florence. This is Chianti Classico territory. In 1978, after a rainy cold spring and a long dry summer, the land produced an excessive number of Cabernet grapes, as it had for a couple of years. We used some of those grapes in our Tignanello, where they were blended with Sangiovese, but we had more than we needed. I decided to make wine from the extra Cabernet grapes on their own, bottle the results, place it all in the cellar, and then wait. We produced 3,600 bottles. The vines were young; no one knew what would happen once the wine had had time to age. Nor were we convinced that the market was ready for a wine from Chianti Classico made only with foreign grapes.

In 1979, there was another exceptional harvest of Cabernet Sauvignon and Cabernet Franc. This time, we decided to go for it. We made the wine, bottled it, waited an appropriate amount of time, and in 1981 we finally were ready to launch our French-Tuscan wine. It was a big success, which encouraged us to sell some of the "experimental" bottles from the previous year that had been aging in the cellars. We continued to invest in the wine and to work on it, adjusting the blend of the two types of grapes.

Anyone who follows the wine business knows the rest of the story. In 1982, we ended up adding an even stronger Tuscan accent to our Cabernet with 20 percent Sangiovese. The result was a fantastic wine prized by collectors and still sold at auction in Italy and abroad. It was a wine with exceptional balance, great finesse, and outstanding potential for aging. Then, in 1997, the spring and summer in Tuscany were exceptionally dry and warm, but not too dry and warm, and the mercury dropped almost imperceptibly in April. The wine from grapes harvested at Solaia that year became available in 2000. It was perfect then, and it still is today. It's no coincidence that that year, for the first time ever, an Italian wine was number one in the annual international rankings in *Wine Spectator*. A $115 Italian wine was on top of the world. A wine created as an experiment had become a collector's item. (Albiera has found that in some places, Solaia costs five times what we charged for it.)

All the way back in 1979, this excellent wine made several significant statements. First, it said that international grapes such as Cabernet Sauvignon and Cabernet Franc that originally came from France but were now being grown in various parts of the world could be used to make a product with a strong connection to the terroir where they had been grown and treated with love. That over time, the climate, soil, and local winemaking traditions would combine to create something unique and different. Later we would see that year as the moment when the "sacred bond" between grape and area of origin, which had characterized—and in some ways hindered—Italian winemaking for centuries, was severed once and for all.

Second, that much-admired Solaia demonstrated that the future belonged to wines that prized elegance over power and that managed to combine drinkability with the capacity to age long and well. Before that, the commonly held belief was that only "big" reds—meaning those that were excessively woody, tannic, and had high acidity—could age without risk. On the contrary, our Solaia offers freshness and sweet, fruity aromas even many years later. Like every wine, it opens and develops, but it does so with grace and harmony, and without losing the strength imparted to it by the fields and the sun. Falling somewhere between past tradition and the promise of the future, it's a wine that has helped change the winemaking world. The name Solaia is ancient, however, and very Tuscan—it's a name that was found on some old maps in the Tignanello archives, marking a place where the exposure to the sun was perfect. Apparently, as far back as the Middle Ages grape growers recognized how important that was.

Born, unplanned, in a lucky September more than thirty harvests ago, perfected with patience and dedication, growing better with time, since then Solaia has aged in the first level of the Tignanello cellars. Its grapes are handpicked one by one and only in the best years. It's a pure distillation of everything we are and everything we do—the modern style of the Antinori cellars, a plant that has been with us for more than half a century. It was sown by my grandfather and my uncle, made strong and fertile by my father, and I am nurturing, drinking, fertilizing, and grafting it.

The Antinori style—our business style and our lifestyle—is made up of many small elements, each one with impact on the ultimate quality of the work. This model, this protocol has been adjusted over the years and passed down through the generations. If I had to reduce this "recipe" for excellence to a series of principles, relying on what I learned from my father and my grandfather, as well as what I've gleaned myself from both successes and failures, I'd start with the letter P, for Patience.

In the early 2000s we worked with our U.S. importers from Chateau Ste. Michelle in Washington State to look for land to plant a completely new vineyard. Allen Shoup, the president of the American company, suggested an area that I didn't know. It was perfect in terms of position and type of soil, sun, and slope. It seemed like a done deal. But at the last minute I learned that the owners wanted to give us a forty-year lease. "We don't think that short-term," I protested. "Forty years won't be long enough for this kind of project." My friends were surprised, as was the journalist from *The Wall Street Journal* who told that story in an April 2008 article (the same one I've already mentioned about the Antinoris as winemakers since the Middle Ages who have been doing business for generations).

Locating the ideal plot of land is only the beginning. It takes three to four years just to begin production. Then it takes another five to six years for the vineyard to become more mature and capable of producing high-quality grapes. Then, especially when we're talking about reds, it takes a minimum of three to four years of aging in the cellar. There are relatively new wines whose reactions to aging we can only guess, so there is a high risk of opening the bottles too soon or too late. There are also vineyards that have been around for ages and produce some renowned wines but are becoming their best selves only now, ten, twenty, even sixty years after they were first cultivated. In his classic *Il Vino Giusto* (*The Right Wine*), Luigi Veronelli writes that a vine "needs three years to yield its first fruit, ten or twelve to gain 'intelligence,' and it is only after twenty to forty years that it becomes transcendent." That gives you an idea of how long it takes to go from the initial investment to sale of a product and a return. And maybe that also helps you see the kind of conflict that naturally arose from the Antinori-Whitbread partnership.

After our agreement, the British could finally count a well-known and universally admired Italian wine brand in their portfolio.

They probably used our name more than once to bring an Italian touch to their image, lending it an aura of nobility and Renaissance legacy, not to mention associating it with a collection of vineyards in the best-known wine areas of the country. They invested, and they expected to see a return on that investment. A series of meetings took place at which I was forced to explain that we needed new hectares to be planted in order to have access to a selection of grapes that would be just barely of sufficient quality for our purposes, but that we still were not able to produce an Antinori-level wine. Or I had to explain that I and my colleagues had decided to leave the precious barrels in our cellars for a few more winters before we sold the wine they contained to turn a profit.

They were concerned not only about the length of time it would take to make wine, but about the unknowns that were clearly incompatible with their management style. For about thirty years, the Whitbread family had seen its company quoted on the London Stock Exchange. I think that was one of the major barriers between us. During the last Vinitaly exhibition, in April 2011, an American journalist—also from *The Wall Street Journal*, I believe—noted our latest sales figures, our expansion, and how we've diversified, and then asked why Antinori has never been listed on the stock exchange, given the numerous invitations to form a partnership with one large company or another that we receive. "You're perfect for the stock market," he insisted.

I explained for perhaps the hundredth time in the last few years, as many other classic Italian brands have launched themselves into the fray, that the mentality of the stock market is incompatible with the slow and meditative business of wine. If you decide to take your company public or give up control of it in any other manner, you become dependent on each and every shareholder, each and every partner. Not to mention the analysts and the observers. You have to justify to them every choice you make and every sum of money you invest. And justifying your choices means planning in black and white when the moves you make will turn into dividends and what those dividends will be, adhering to standardized parameters that draw no distinction between great wines and ball bearings.

That's impossible in my world. A vineyard that I begin to cultivate today, choosing plants and trying different varieties, may only yield its best results under the direction of my grandchild. As my daughter Albiera likes to say, "You can't force nature." In one place, we may try three, four, or five different things and then choose to continue with only one. Or we may decide to make major changes to a vineyard that is working well because we have a long-term plan to make it even better. Then there are the wines like Tignanello—if one year it seems like we're not going to have enough, we simply don't make it. A winemaker who is seeking perfection weighs uncountable priorities and risks when inspecting a new plot of land and considering what can be created there. The potential of a vineyard, as I've already said, cannot be measured objectively based on the slope of the hills and the chemical composition of the soil. The harmony of the surrounding landscape, its history, and the human side of things have no relationship to the stock market; those are matters of instinct and heart.

There is a basic tension between two alien worlds that I came to understand during the Whitbread era. Those were the years when globalization was changing everything—the size of the market, the image of Italian wine, and the way it was distributed. And it was that first and only experience with dividing up the company that made me see how I wanted us to do our work, both in terms of time and in terms of style. And I understood, too, how I *did not* want us to work. So I always say no to the bank groups that periodically make sky-high offers for stakes in the company, telling me that "We'll never see a market like this again" and "It will never be worth more."

I give the same response to the management companies that come up with three-year plans to increase our exports. I can't believe that anything important or lasting can be done in three years, and I think we have all the resources we need to develop our strategies in-house. For that reason, I take pride in the fact that in fifty years of running the company, even in the most difficult times, I've never had to resort to distributing dividends (or laying people off, even temporarily).

There was a specific moment in the 1980s when our general incompatibility with our English partners started to become clear. My colleagues and I thought it was time to expand grape production. Basically, we needed new vineyards. And then, shortly thereafter, two interesting opportunities arose. Interesting to us, that is.

The first was an offer to acquire Pèppoli in 1985. This is a vineyard five kilometers from Tignanello, in *the heart of the heart* of Chianti Classico country, the kingdom of the Sangiovese grape, where Vallumbrosan monks have been making wine since the Middle Ages. This place has a long-standing relationship with my family and our cellars: for centuries we bought grapes there. In the name of those historical ties, the owners offered us the entire estate—a small sunny valley with mineral-rich soil—under decidedly advantageous conditions. After the monks, the land had been owned by the Cerchi, Ridolfi, and Saccardi families, all Florentine dynasties famous for a knack for business and a love for and appreciation of beauty, but also for violence and audacity. We would become the new owners exactly six hundred years after a member of our family had joined the vintners' guild.

The second piece of land we were eyeing was Badia a Passignano. This was another excellent opportunity to increase the quality and prestige of our Chianti wine collection, and it was very close to the Tignanello land. What matters most in these situations is gut instinct—not what appears on a financial statement or how soon we expect a return on our investment. The San Michele Arcangelo monastery has sat on a low rocky plateau in the center of that land since 1050. This monastery was built atop the foundation of an even older building and was built at the direction of the founder of the Vallumbrosan order, Saint John Gualbert. Today, the monks in his order still live in the same rooms, while my family has restored and uses the ancient wine cellars and their two thousand oak casks.

For centuries the Vallumbrosans have practiced diplomacy, even serving as mediators in the conflicts between Siena and Florence. Some of the greatest theologians of their time have worked here. And the art of wine was no less important to this place. It was actually the monks who first nurtured and studied what we now call "Chianti wine." The local Vallumbrosan wine has long been highly regarded, and in 1983 a fossil of a *Vitis vinifera* plant determined to be at least ten thousand years old—the oldest grape in Italy—was discovered in nearby San Vivaldo. This monastery is home to Domenico Ghirlandaio's fresco of the Last Supper, which depicts a couple of glasses of wine sitting on the table in front of the apostles. Here, too, the great Tuscan scientist Galileo Galilei taught mathematics and sought to unravel the mysteries of the universe. And here, as we've already seen, probably in the very cold winter of 1179, a monk and an Antinori met to handle the sale of goods and land. Our name was written for the first time ever on a parchment that is now preserved in the archives in Badia a Ripoli.

These things have no value on a stock exchange. Nor do the personal memories that those ancient walls called up for me. A photo from 1890 that my father kept in Palazzo Antinori shows the silhouette of the abbey in the hills, with its fortified towers and the small town surrounding it. It's the backdrop for a group of friends dressed in swank hunting gear passing around a flask. That same tower and dark cloud of cypress trees, a symbol to me of the serenity and poetry of my beloved Tuscany, jutted above the horizon that I stared at through my window in Santa Cristina a Tignanello, where we had evacuated during the dark days of the war.

It was immediately clear that it would take a lot of work to make the land in both Pèppoli and Badia a Passignano suitable for modern viticulture. In the pragmatic terms that Whitbread would have used, it was going to require a huge investment. During the years when the English were trying to get new shares from me in order to take control of the company, I suggested acquiring two large pieces of land without even saying when a drinkable wine could be expected and, as a result, when a profit could be turned. Basically, my partners and their little army of managers could not understand this transaction in economic terms. They could not see a guaranteed return on investment. That return on investment is calculated using a specific formula based on the capital invested.

They explained to me that rather than worrying about vineyards and abbeys, old casks and fifteenth-century frescoes, I could increase the value of the company by reducing the yield. In financial terms, what I wanted to do didn't make any sense.

How did it end? I ignored their unhappiness and their cautions to be prudent and to move slowly. In 1985, we bought Pèppoli, and today, twenty years later, we make organic extra-virgin olive oil and one of our best-selling Chianti Classico wines there. In 1987, we acquired Badia a Passignano. Right now in its cellars, under cross vaults that have darkened over the years, Badia a Passignano Riserva, our signature Chianti Classico, is aging in small oak barrels. We've also opened an enoteca and an osteria there. It was the right choice, but I was beginning to feel the winds of disapproval blowing my way from London.

Patience. Lately I've realized that the slow and thoughtful pace of grape growing and winemaking are a real challenge to the frantic rhythms of today. Albiera often says this when she's giving a talk of some kind: "Today, we have high-speed airplanes and high-speed trains, and thoughts and words travel just as quickly on the Web. But wine still develops at the same pace. You can't make it go any faster." Indeed, wine is slow. It evolves gradually. And it should be tasted slowly. A high-quality bottle produced by someone who learned to walk before he learned to run will last much longer than any trend and will be good long after the latest smartphone is outmoded. There are new car models. Governments come and go. Even the climate is changing. But wine ages without changing its essence.

Just as you may change in some ways but you always remain your essential self, so does wine. You may open it and find that it's mature, but also as energetic and fresh as when it was bottled. For modern sensibilities, wine is a provocation. Surely this is part of its charm.

Another P, a classic Tuscan trait: Perseverance. Tenacity. The obstinacy of farmers. That's how, in the 1800s, they triumphed over vine disease and other problems that had decimated our vineyards. It was a farmer from Pisa, "trying and trying again" (as the motto of the Accademia del Cimento, founded in 1657 by a group of Florentine scientists, goes), who conquered the plague of mildew, treating his vines with sulphur and soap. And others rebuilt our vineyards after defeating the scourge of the grape phylloxera, root-eating insects that arrived like marauding hordes on ships from America and brought the countryside of the Old World to its knees.

Without "trying and trying again," there would be no Tignanello or Solaia today. Without perseverance, we would not have rebuilt our wine cellars on top of the rubble and shards after World War II. My father's study in Palazzo Antinori—which smells of wood and old carpets, and which has remained unchanged since his death—would be the workspace of some bank loan officer. Without perseverance, we would never have left Tuscany to sell our wines in markets where consumers didn't know who we were and what we'd been doing for centuries. "No, thanks, we don't need any dishes," a restaurant owner in Avellino once said in the 1960s as he gave me the brush-off, perhaps confusing Antinori with Ginori, a Florentine ceramics company. (He probably didn't realize that the Ginori store in the center of Florence is just a few doors down from Palazzo Antinori.) You need to push forward, figure out the problem, and design a plan to counteract it. (For example, not wanting anyone to mistake me ever again for a maker of tableware, in Campania we then handed the sales of our products over to the Mastrobernardino family, who did an excellent job and today produce their own magnificent local wines under their own name.)

Try and try again. I remember fondly one of my father's daring experiments. After the war, much of his energy was dedicated to finding a new audience and new markets abroad and at home. He was a self-taught marketing genius, and one day he came up with the idea of a bottle in the shape of a fish. It was outlandish—a toy that would get the attention of people who didn't know anything about wine denominations and decanters. "We need to work on packaging," he used to say all the time. He was one of the first to stop using the straw-covered Chianti bottles that had been on local osteria tables for at least seven centuries. The fish bottle—I saw one recently in the window of an antique shop—was a big success in America.

I started to suspect, however, that we'd taken a wrong turn a short time later when I was at border control at an American airport and someone working there read my name on my passport and said, "Oh, the fish bottle!" I wasn't flattered. I felt like I'd taken a shortcut that had nothing to do with quality to gaining recognition for the brand. I'd much rather have heard, "Oh, Antinori! You make those fantastic Tuscan wines!" Since then, we've left the fish in the aquarium. Now, everything from labels to advertising is simple and uncluttered. Still, I have to admire my father's ongoing efforts to try new things, with little inhibition and a lot of creativity.

Another memory of my father: one of the first times I went on a sales call with him, when I was just observing, an afternoon many years ago in Rome. There were two names on the list. The first was the elderly Commendatore Gabbrielli, owner of Buton, the largest wine store in the Italian capital city, near the Trevi Fountain. I remember the small glasses of sherry that he would give each of his visitors, and his advanced age. My father explained to me that it was crucial to have his support in order to get our name into the places that counted in the capital. That was one of my first lessons in "wine diplomacy."

Our second appointment in Rome was even more important. We were meeting with a Mr. De Corné. He was the Italian director of the Compagnie Internationale des Wagon-Lits, a very proper businessman whom I got to know better after I'd climbed up the ladder. At that time, being on the wine lists of the dining cars that crisscrossed the continents—which were true restaurants—was very prestigious. My father was determined to have his wines sold on those trains.

A protracted struggle between my father and De Corné ensued. Because of his personality or because he had been directed to do so, over the course of many long and exhausting visits, he proved highly resistant to admitting us into that closed circle of suppliers. Years passed. There were seemingly infinite visits to that office in Rome. And then, finally, we did it. We got the news that our bottles would be included on that esteemed list of wines available on the railway.

My father decided to celebrate this victory in style. He organized a train trip with several of his friends. He seated himself in the dining car and in a loud voice ordered a bottle of his own wine from the waiter. Upon hearing the order, the waiter looked uncomfortable. He leaned down and very discreetly whispered in my father's ear, "Listen, you don't want that. I've heard it's made with apples." I don't know exactly how that particular meal ended, but I know that even then, my father didn't give up. This story shows that making good wine is just the first step. It doesn't mean anything if you don't manage to let people know about it. And it shows that you need a thick skin and great tolerance toward competitors who can't bring themselves to applaud your success.

Planning—a third P—is the only tool that can be used to deal with the unknowable aspects of wine. You till soil, plant vines, schedule harvests. You have the cellars all ready, filled with new barrels and bottles. And then something goes wrong. It's inevitable. Until we grow grapes in laboratories (something I sincerely hope will never come to pass), they will be grown among rocks and soil, under the sky, exposed to the environment, their flavor distilled and developed by scorching sun and pouring rain, frosts and full moons, storms and clear skies. Too much heat destabilizes the sugars. An early frost ruins the growth. Too much sun, too little sun, too much rain, and no rain at all. Hail and snow are okay until early spring, but once the clusters are growing fat on the vine they're disastrous. There's good wind that clears the air and dries the rain and dew, and bad wind that bends the vines, strips them of their leaves, breaks them, and blows them away.

There are thousands of unknowns in the very delicate stage of aging, and there's always a chance of excessive precipitation. Winemaking is a long process, and even with today's science and technology, parts of it remain mysterious—that's the beauty of it. In the end, you have a glass that's either a miracle or a disappointment.

I think a good winemaker has to be part psychologist, with himself as the patient. He has to face failure, draw strength from success, accept with serenity the parts of his work that he cannot change. Planning means keeping a stock of wine—and a minimum level of economic resources—for years that don't go well, whether it's due to a dry summer, a harsh winter, or a poorly performing market. Prudence means that you still think like a farmer, even when your fields are located on three different continents. You need to keep your eye on everything at once, so that sometimes you focus on one thing and sometimes on another, depending on the situation. A long-term outlook means always having a plan B.

In a very rainy 2002, when we went to harvest the grapes in Tignanello we found that most of them hadn't ripened properly and had practically rotted on the vine. What does a winemaker concerned with quality do in this situation? We skipped a year. Most of the grapes, especially our beloved Sangiovese grapes, which are late bloomers and sensitive to dampness, went unused.

Instead, we made our Solaia "Annata Diversa" ("Different Vintage," as we say in technical jargon), with Cabernet Sauvignon and Cabernet Franc grapes. Experts described the wine as "intense, rich, and elegant," which is high praise for something that came about almost by accident. That year and in 1992, another bad year when everything seemed to go wrong, we were the only ones who decided not to bottle the "stars" in our catalogue, even though it would do financial damage. No Tignanello, no Guado al Tasso in Bolgheri, no Chianti Classico Riserva. The spring of 2011 was also strange, with high temperatures in early April and then a cold snap. The heat opened the buds, but then the cold halted their progress. We didn't know until 2013 what kind of wine we'd get out of that unusual weather. It turned out to have a good concentration, soft tannins, and slightly lower acidity than the wine of previous years. As for the unknowns of the market, just think of the out-of-nowhere hailstorm that is the recent recession from which we are just now finally and slowly recovering. It came from America, just like phylloxera, and it's had an effect all over the world. I believe in something I call "the rule of ten," meaning that while there is never any lack of difficult moments and delays, these kinds of serious problems come around once every decade. I'm not just talking about the weather either.

There were a couple of acquisitions made after I took charge of the company in 1966 that turned out to be more damaging than any rainy summer. First, there was the Northeast. Our importers in the United States had reported to us many times that there was growing demand for Veneto wines, especially Soave and Valpolicella. The white Soave made by the Bolla family had become a status symbol imbibed by movie stars. Frank Sinatra was said not to eat unless there was a bottle of it at the right temperature on his table. I decided to buy the Santi company, which had worked in the Verona area with Soave, Valpolicella, and Amarone for a long time. It was a hasty decision, and I saw pretty quickly that I had made a mistake.

Their vineyards and their whole system were unstable. I remember that I had to go up there at least every two weeks to check on the progress of restoring the land. I had to confront the old owner, who seemed to lack the sincere dedication and passion needed for the new and difficult wine market. I had to assign Paolo Perissinotto, a great lover of wine whom I'd known for some time, to oversee the project. That was the only positive thing to come out of that troubled time.

In previous years, as director of sales for Azienda Santa Margherita, Perissinotto had made Pinot Grigio, until then a somewhat banal wine, a phenomenon. It was his brilliant idea to apply classic white-wine making techniques to the "coppery" grapes of the Triveneto area. If his name has not been recorded in the history books, it is only because he's a modest person who doesn't toot his own horn. That's probably why I liked him so much. But not even he could save that company, and soon Santi was nothing but a burden to us. It was a black hole that sucked in our resources and energy.

Then I made a move in Umbria, in the Orvieto area, where my father had begun slowly acquiring land in the white grape regions, with an eye to adding a white wine to our collection of big Tuscan reds. Florentine Giancarlo Cassi made a good offer to sell us his Cantine Bigi, an historic local company that seemed perfect for our purposes. Here, too, however, we soon saw that we would need to do a lot of work on the infrastructure before we could get started. Tachis, my trusted enologist, and I began to think about a completely new winemaking facility. It was to be one of Italy's most advanced for producing white wines. This was exciting, but the costs kept rising. I had been running Antinori for a short time and I had already discovered that being a winemaker could cause a lot of sleepless nights, to put it mildly. These deals were not merely follies due to youthful impetuousness; they were disasters. The future of my family's company was hanging in the balance, and the banks were lying in wait.

The appearance of Alberto De Marchi was a stroke of luck. He was a key figure in the sale of Italian wines after World War II. I met him in Belgium, where he was running his own company, during my first tour as the Antinori spokesperson in Europe. De Marchi, which had begun as a small wine sales operation, had risen to the top of Wine Food (today known as the Gruppo Italiano Vini). Thanks to large amounts of Swiss capital, that group had begun to take over prestigious Italian winemakers that were in trouble, saving them from extinction. Fortunately, De Marchi wanted to buy both Santi and Bigi. We quickly reached an agreement, and we could breathe again.

I'd learned my lesson. What had gone wrong? Maybe I hadn't been well enough informed about the real potential of the markets or hadn't done a good job of calculating whether we had enough funds to be up to the task. In other words, I had failed at planning. If one good thing was to come out of my partnership with the English, it was that I learned to do rigorous accounting, and to pay attention to return on investment and day-to-day management. I'll never be driven by the stock exchange. Before investing, I'll always first consider the wine that I could make, and then look at market trends. But working side by side with an international corporation listed on the stock exchange would teach me to think a lot harder and to look before I leapt, which was what I had failed to do with the Veneto project.

You might even say that we weren't ready to venture out from Tuscany into such different territory. That we were impatient. Or even that I had hastily looked for a shortcut to get around the slow-moving ways of wine. I'd committed the sin of arrogance. The human factor plays its part, too. The audience has an impact. Fashions in wine change, they evolve, they turn on a dime. Just think of the boom in barrels, which would have such an influence on our fate. At first, those oak barrels were scorned, and then they came to be considered miraculous amphorae in which mediocre wine could be transformed into something as wondrous as the wine at the marriage at Cana. Or think of the rage for Novello, inspired by French Beaujolais Nouveau, which is made with a specific kind of fermentation that's light and unstable and needs to be consumed right away. For a few years nobody talked about anything else. Don't even get me started on sparkling wine on tap.

These are sudden changes in taste that can eat up years of investment in a short time. How do you predict the next wave? Just as the grapes need to interact with the climate, the troposphere, and the environment, winemakers who aim to make high-quality wines must be part of society and be out in the world.

You need to travel, stay informed, talk to people, keep up to date. Basically, you need to be interested, stimulated by everything that's happening around your business. And you need to love wine. A winemaker who fails to drink at least one glass a day for pleasure, who doesn't experience wine frequently, everywhere from the humble restaurant on the corner to the wine bar of a fancy hotel, in short, a winemaker who never leaves the cellar, is like a chef who has never tasted his own dishes and never goes to restaurants or grocery stores. Never trust a thin chef! You have to be both producer and consumer. Year after year, this allows you to be in tune with the market and with people's tastes. Each era has its own concept of good wine. You have to understand what that is. Today, Hollywood stars like Tom Cruise and Robert De Niro and even Francis Ford Coppola (so passionate about wine that he now has his own vineyard in Napa Valley) no longer have bottles of Soave on their tables. Our Solaia and Tignanello sit there in its place.

There is yet another P: Precision. Growing grapes requires a method. Nothing can be done on the fly. The modern winemaker must know how each type of grape will react to the land. Precision winemaking means being able to control how the use of a cluster of grapes from the center or the outside of the row, ten meters lower or ten meters higher on the side of a hill, will influence the end result. The same is true of dozens of infinitesimal variations in the composition of the soil, the degree of humidity, and the angle of the sun. In practice, you need to know every single vineyard and each parcel—each specific section of the vineyard—and their schedules and characteristics. You have to know how they change over time, how they react to the seasons and to changes in the weather. You have to know each and every plant personally and follow every phase of the work involved. The posts that support the vines and when and how to prune must be conscious choices. You have to think carefully about the casks—no two are the same, and you need to taste from all of them—the bottles, and the color of the glass (another of Giacomo Tachis's obsessions), the cork, the label.

A winemaker's precision is a mix of perfectionism and practice. It's nurtured by new scientific discoveries about soil chemistry and microbiology and uses new high-tech methods; today, with remote sensing, I can adjust fertilizer and other treatments based on the health of each individual plant. We've acquired the most modern "intelligent machines" on the market for our vineyards, and created new integrated systems for managing warehouses, archives, labels, and even vines.

But a winemaker's precision sticks to tradition, too, to the gestures, rites, and knowledge that have been developed over centuries—the fundamental things that make your wine recognizable and give it a rich identity. In many cases we still apply the same practices that my winemaking ancestors used. In Tignanello, the green grapes for vin santo (the Tuscan dessert wine that was used during Mass for centuries) are still spread out by hand on a wooden grid. It takes forty people two days to do this. Often these are the children and grandchildren of the farmers who originally worked the land. When it comes to harvesting grapes, an experienced farmer's look, touch, and smell are priceless.

A lot of people aren't aware that the harvest of grapes for big reds is performed in about fifteen days by going up and down the same rows. There are so many bunches of grapes in a single vineyard, and they ripen at different times. They have to be picked at just the right moment. Frequently the grapes higher up on the plant are harvested first, and then those closer to the ground are picked a few days later. They really need to be examined one by one.

White grapes, on the other hand, need to be picked and processed at a low temperature. The harvest begins at dawn or during the night so that the air will be cool, and it all depends on the weather and how the season has gone. Those are things no machine can understand.

Today the reach of technology extends to new packaging and new materials, but I believe a wine bottle must always be made of glass. I'm not interested in cans or Tetra Paks! I use only natural cork, which "kisses" the wine as it ages. Anything different would take away some of the value and charm of the finished product. The cork arrives in unfinished form, some from Portugal, but mainly from Sardinia. With the University of Cagliari and some other winemakers, we've developed a project to replenish the woods near Nuoro by planting five thousand cork oak trees. Under the guise of corporate social responsibility, we're bringing back an ancient tradition, with the added benefit of decreasing the amount of CO_2 in the atmosphere.

Precision and respect for tradition don't mean that wine follows strict rules, or that everything has been predetermined. A wine-maker should never be an accountant with no room for imagination. The ability to take advantage of opportunities, the instinct to think on one's feet, intuition, creativity—these are all very important (even if they don't start with the letter P). An example? Once in the late 1960s, I was having dinner with our Milan salespeople at a restaurant outside of the city. The main dining room sported a row of brand-new wine barrels. When the owner realized who I was, he asked me if he could have some wine to put in them, in order to be able to tap them one day in honor of his customers, just as taverns traditionally did at one time.

It was an unusual request. We hadn't really worked with unbottled wine for a hundred years or more. But we wanted to keep up a good relationship with the restaurant—highly regarded at the time—and since it didn't seem too difficult, I helped him out. A few days later, I had enough Chianti Classico Villa Antinori to fill his barrels delivered to the restaurant. Then, two or three years later, I returned. Naturally, I was curious to find out what had happened to that wine. I was pretty sure it had been compromised by sitting in those barrels—probably oxidized with a high degree of volatile acidity. In layman's terms, undrinkable. What a surprise it was to discover that the wine had aged better in those barrels than it had in the traditional way! It would be a stretch to say that that's where I got the idea of aging wine in barrels, which was not common in Italy at the time, but it certainly made me think. When I started to consider how best to age the new Tuscan wines, that experience was still on my mind.

Pretty far down the list of words beginning with P, we arrive at Profit. My father taught me that earnings, sales, and expansion are not our ultimate goal. They're a part of the business, for sure. But profit is just proof of efficiency. It confirms that your wines were produced the right way, meet the needs of customers, and are better than your competitors' wines. That's why you can sell your wine at what you think is the right price. Profit is necessary for survival: only a good bottom line can protect you from bad years and financial crises, fluctuation in demand and rifts in the company. Profit also guarantees independence, because with it you don't have to seek assistance from others. It lets you try new things and take a long-term view. For all these reasons, profit is a driver for improvement. Without economic resources, a company cannot perform research, cannot work on its materials or its structure or the tools that it uses. A company needs profit to continue evolving, following the market, the changing world, and its own inspiration.

An example of compromise between profit and quality? I haven't mentioned Galestro much here, but for a long time in the 1980s and 1990s, this wine—which takes its name from a local stone—was our top seller. It was a light white wine that people enjoyed in the summer, and it expanded our business quickly.

It all began with a group project. Several Tuscan companies joined together to find a use for the excess of white grapes (Trebbiano in particular) produced in the region and previously used to make Chianti—with disastrous results. The Galestro line—Capsula Viola was the most successful—experienced a boom, but it was a wine that could not possibly aspire to the quality I was seeking, given its raw material. Furthermore, the market ballooned, especially in Italy, and our vineyards were soon not up to producing enough grapes. We began to purchase grapes from other vineyards.

The result was millions of bottles that sold, but that represented a step backward along the route I had mapped with my father: following the process from plant to cellar, striving for quality, and never making wines that would merely quench someone's thirst. On the other hand, the profits from Galestro were immediately reinvested, which allowed us to grow stronger and attempt a lot of new initiatives around the world in the following decade. Galestro did well. It was insurance for our future, the kind of thing I'd needed during the Soave and Valpolicella situation. Now that it has fallen out of favor, we make one fifth of what we made back then.

How do I see that experience in retrospect? Renzo Cotarella, who knows me and has worked with me for thirty years and calls me every day, no matter where he is, just to tell me if it's raining or the sun is shining on our vineyards, once told me that I'm a businessman with a strong commercial instinct and an equally strong love of production and the search for the perfect wine. My father, even more than I, managed to live that same passion and participate in both parts of the business. Unlike many of his colleagues, friends, and farmers, he understood that sometimes it's smarter to delegate production in order to dedicate yourself to other aspects.

Many Tuscan winemakers, especially those from aristocratic families, though sincere lovers of wine, preferred to stay on their estates and watch the vines grow. They found the commercial side of the business undignified. They didn't take an interest in sales of grapes or the sale and distribution of bottles, most of which didn't bear their names. They made wine because it was traditional to do so—a sort of high-class hobby—but they didn't want to be associated with it by name. It was the opposite of the way things work today, when so many people make wine only to feed their egos by seeing their names on the bottles.

My grandfather had already gotten over this psychological threshold. More specifically, Piero and Lodovico Antinori split everything up: the former was better at sales and the latter was more interested in production. But it was my father, a former salesperson of medical products, who was the first to be involved in all aspects of the business and to represent everything to do with the wine. He was the first to understand that high-quality wine is the only kind of wine that can help a company grow steadily and over the long term, and that kind of wine can only be made as the result of a cycle in which every phase is important. The purchasing of the land, the planting of the grapes, the density of the vines and their clusters, the cellar, the actual making of the wine, the image, planning, and distribution—there's no point in having one without the others.

More and more the work of the business is divided up between Albiera, Allegra, and Alessia. But all three sisters have at least "tasted" the various parts of the business. I've always felt pulled in both directions. In general, in recent years Marchesi Antinori is trying to unite these often conflicting forces: quality without compromise cultivated on increasingly solid foundations. That explains the acquisition of new land, and the planning of new facilities. It's all part of the eternal search for balance.

In conclusion, I'd add that awards, rankings, and headlines are only a means toward a more complex and difficult goal. I've never been enthusiastic about advertising. We've never invested in television commercials, and we don't spend much on print advertising either. And we choose our sponsorships more with our hearts than with our heads.

This all raises a question: What's the point? Why work so hard? If profit, market growth, and greater visibility are only tools, what's the point of trying to achieve the ideal wine—a transcendental wine, as Veronelli put it—that I and my ancestors and my family members and my coworkers focus on every day? I've thought about that a lot and I've thought about what my father used to say. My conclusion is that thinking about wine, updating the cellars, refining our wines, and acquiring new vineyards are all about leaving a better company for the next generation than the one I inherited. Knowing that I am an active part of Tuscan winemaking means knowing that I have not wasted my time. The family company works not if the status quo is preserved, but if it continues to improve. If the future is approached with passion. My father managed to do that despite two world wars. I have it easier than he did, and I hope to do it, too.

The final P stands for Passion. I'm talking about passion for what we do and everything it represents. It's a way of approaching all of life. It can be seen not only in the final product, but in the way we live.

Passion is a very Mediterranean and very Tuscan concept. Foreigners are charmed by Italy and my region in particular because beauty and harmony—in craftsmanship, in art, in a simple dish of beans dressed with extra-virgin olive oil—are not the work of a single creative and enterprising mind, but the continuous and natural output of a system. As an Italian winemaker—and the same goes for Italian chefs, restaurateurs, designers, artists—I generate beauty and quality because I've been taught to do so and raised among them and I recognize them around me in the cities and in the countryside. I renew my commitment to them every time I sit down at a table or choose an object.

In our specific system of beauty and quality, which I think is a distinguishing feature of the Antinori style, wine is the ever-present background and the focus. But there's more than wine in my family tree. I have ancestors who were literati and warriors, archbishops and ambassadors, from Brindisi to Milan. There were diplomats and administrators in the Florentine Republic and the Grand Duchy of the Medici family, the reign of the Lorraine family and the new bureaucracy of the Savoys in the modern era. I come from a dynasty with far-reaching roots in culture and politics in various eras. Many Antinoris have played their part in history.

In the late fifteenth century, Tommaso Antinori was one of the wise men at the trial of Girolamo Savonarola, the Dominican monk who rocked the city by preaching against the Church and the order, and who was hung and burned in Piazza della Signoria. (For the record, Tommaso voted for absolution.) A generation later, Amerigo di Camillo was the head of a faction that rebelled against the Medicis, an exile and mercenary leader with changing fortunes whose father had to spring him from prison more than once. This long-haired Antinori from more than five hundred years ago will look out at us forever from a portrait by Jacopo Carucci, known as Pontormo.

Alessandro, son of Niccolò, was director of Ufficio del Monte, the first Italian bank, around 1550. Bastiano was a founder in the sixteenth century of the Accademia della Crusca, which defends the purity of Italian language. Vincenzio, born in the late 1700s, was a well-known academic and scientist. Among other things, he was an illustrious member of the Accademia dei Georgofili, one of the first bodies in Italy involved in the science of land and agriculture, and served as curator of the writings of Galileo Galilei, the man who plucked planet Earth from the center of the solar system (he wasn't burned at the stake, but he was placed under house arrest), and of Alessandro Volta, father of the electric battery. Antinoris have been dancers at court and players of *calcio fiorentino* (the violent Renaissance sport that was the forerunner of today's soccer), not to mention poets and writers.

I've always been intrigued by Bernardino di Antonio di Raffaello Antinori, a poet and courtier in the sixteenth century. He specialized in poetry lauding local noblewomen, and he is said to have composed one poem too many for Bianca Cappello, the blond and much-discussed second wife of Francesco I de' Medici. The jealous grand duke had him imprisoned, and he was almost certainly killed in prison. Other sources tell a different story, namely that a Bernardo Antinori had an affair with Dianora di Toledo, who was the wife of another son of Cosimo's, the ferocious Pietro, and the niece of the elegant grand duchess Eleonora di Toledo (shown in a Bronzino portrait wearing an incredible black, white, and gold outfit). But the ending is the same: he was condemned to prison and death by a jealous husband because of a beautiful woman.

Many of my ancestors were lovers of art. In the late seventeenth century, Palazzo Antinori acquired a sublime *Madonna con San*

Giuseppe e San Giovannino by Raphael. Two centuries later, Egisto Fabbri, my grandfather's brother-in-law, had the foresight to purchase sixteen Paul Cézanne canvases back when the Impressionist genius was not yet well-known. We are quite proud that Piero Antinori was friends with Puccini, a great musician, a great Tuscan, and, like the Antinoris, a curious world traveler and hunter. He was especially fond of hunting birds from a boat on the canals around Massaciuccoli Lake. It's said that Piero Antinori told the composer, a native of Lucca, about a play he'd seen in the United States, David Belasco's *The Girl of the Golden West*, which inspired Puccini to write his famous opera *La Fanciulla del West*.

Still today, we lead very full lives, totally engaged and dedicated to the system of beauty and good living that is the Tuscan and Italian lifestyle. You won't find a single member of my family who's a government minister or the CEO of a big corporation. Most of our energy goes into our bottles, but we always try to contribute to the wine world as a whole, while promoting Florence and Tuscany wherever we can. Opportunities for me to use my Tuscan-accented English abound. I have fewer chances to use my French, which I studied for years and which was once the main language of wine; today I use it mostly in my work with the University of Bordeaux.

Our love of art can be seen in the initiatives of the Accademia Antinori, which was designed to support and publicize artists, artwork, and projects related to our wine and our rural landscape. One family favorite is Egisto Ferroni, a naturalist painter from Lastra a Signa, who painted large and lively canvases depicting the vineyards and fieldwork traditions of the last century. In 2002, we helped to have a cycle of eight of his works restored and exhibited in Livorno. He was a pioneer who staunchly defended the excessive realism of his subjects against the criticism of his contemporaries, and preferred his isolated studio in the fields to the drawing rooms of Livorno and Florence. In 2007, we organized an exhibit of wine vessels from ancient Greece that was held in the courtyard of Palazzo Antinori. On display were fifteen-hundred-year-old pieces from the National Archaeological Museum in Florence that originated in Cyprus and the Aegean. We also held a contemporary art exhibit on the theme of wine, and we've been involved with numerous other initiatives. The one most dear to me was a selection of photographs from the Alinari Archives exhibited in Palazzo Antinori in 2003. It included two hundred century-old photos of our land in Chianti, Maremma, Mugello, Valdichiana, and elsewhere, images of farmers and seasonal workers in the vineyards, picnics in the woods, and carts pulled by light-colored Maremmana cattle with their long horns.

Between harvests, I and my daughters have always found time to stay outside, and to play sports. We do this partly for health reasons, of course, but it's also in our genes to love the outdoors, nature, and the land where we grew up. My grandfather Piero was the first president of the Italian Tennis Federation, founded on May 18, 1910, at the Florence Tennis Club in Cascine Park. (These days Alessia is the family tennis star.)

I spent my youth on a bicycle. My father, who loved both the beach and the mountains, and who traveled Holland by bike later in life, liked nothing more than taking his children on long bike rides. I recall thrilling trips through Val d'Aosta, Abruzzo, and practically every road and path in Tuscany, places I would later ride with my own children. We also traveled days and days in the saddles of some of the earliest mopeds.

Horses are a big part of our lives as well. Allegra has built a stable of thoroughbreds at the Macchia del Bruciato in Guado al Tasso. Albiera has competed in the ring and she does a half hour of practice at the center in Cascine in the morning. She also likes to promote horseback riding as a sport that offers useful training for both life and style. "Horseback riding and business have a lot in common," she often says. Perhaps that's why rather than giving my granddaughter Verdiana a typical harvest initiation into the business, she sent her to work as a groom in the United States to pay her dues.

One of our family traditions for several centuries has been hunting, as you can see from the hoofed trophies hanging on the walls of the house in Guado al Tasso, as well as many paintings depicting hunting scenes. Many of them were painted by Eugenio Cecconi, a post-Macchiaiolo (the Macchiaiolo movement was a Florentine Impressionist movement) from Livorno who was a great friend of my grandfather Piero's and a terrific hunter.

In addition to being a hunter, my father was an avid photographer who left us many black-and-white photos that bear witness to the Tuscan Maremma area of an earlier time. He hunted often with me in and around the hills of Tignanello. My daughter Albiera and I hunted together in Guado al Tasso with our dogs Doc and Cyrok. She's carrying on the tradition today in Maremma with her own kids.

I've become a solitary hunter, though, and I shoot infrequently. I've hunted in Africa, Austria, and elsewhere, but these days I prefer to stay close to home. Renzo Cotarella is a lot like me. We both like to go out on our own, so we split up the hunting grounds. He leaves at dawn for the hills of Umbria, known for white truffles, in view of Castello della Sala. I prefer the pine woods in Bolgheri and the fields and swamps in Guado al Tasso. Renzo and I love the silence of nature, wandering off the trail, being alone with our dogs. It's all part of the experience of hunting, and any good hunter knows that whether or not you shot a pheasant is the least important thing at the end of the day.

The last few generations of Antinoris have had a lot of dogs, perhaps because we've tended to spend a lot of time outside of Florence. We used to give the dogs and horses names that began with A, such as Asterix and Asso, a little obsession of mine. (Albiera broke the rules by calling her dog Zulù. After that, all hell broke loose when it came to naming.)

We also frequently give our dogs wine-related names: in Castello della Sala, Alessia had a Dalmatian named Bricco (meaning jug) and a German shepherd named Cork. Even I, to break the chain of A names, have given my beloved German shorthaired pointer the name Doc. He is a purebred hunting dog, so his name isn't that far outside of our usual system even though it doesn't start with an A, because it does relate to wine—it stands for Denominazione di Origine Controllata, or "Controlled Designation of Origin," the official certification of high-quality wines.

When I took the helm of the company, I was young and inexperienced. But I already knew well how passion permeates everything: work, family, art, social commitment, travel, sports, hunting, dogs, horses. And most of all wine. This is what nurtures our approach and guides us through life, what fuels the patience and perseverance, precision and creativity. I wanted our wines to be an expression of all that: a certain approach to life, the lifestyle of my family, which I was now charged with representing in the flesh. The missions abroad, putting forth my face and the family name, had already helped me grasp the deep meaning of the family business and my own role in it. Our style is based on the combination of the brand and family history. Our products and their image rest on those things as well. They guarantee lasting quality.

For all these reasons, having the name Antinori is as much an honor as it is a responsibility. Both preparation and passion, as well as personal engagement, count. The leader of a winemaking company must be like the owner of a tavern: customers keep coming back because they know his name—and probably the name of his father and even his grandfather before him. They know he won't water down their wine or serve them a poor vintage. You need to take care of your name and protect it.

To illustrate our philosophy of having direct contact with people who drink and love wine, I show anyone who comes to see me in Florence the small window—more of a peephole, really—that is the exact size of a Tuscan flask. Through it, my ancestors sold wine from the cellars of Palazzo Antinori to passersby as recently as two centuries ago. My father, who brought Villa Antinori into the wine cellars of the most prestigious restaurants and hotels in the world, once again instated a direct line from producer to consumer by opening the Cantinetta Antinori restaurant and wine bar on the ground floor, right across from our meeting room. Today, we sell more bottles every year—six out of ten outside of Italy. We've opened Cantinetta branches in Zurich, Vienna, and Moscow. We're working to win over new markets and new generations.

That's also why I've never stopped traveling since the time we first shipped wine into areas where wine wasn't yet very commonly served. About half of my work hours are dedicated to travel. Traveling is how my father found his path, and it helps me follow in his footsteps. Albiera, Allegra, and Alessia travel for the same reasons. Having members of the family present in the places where our wine is produced and sold means everything. This is one thing you cannot delegate.

Our last name and the way we represent it to the world provide an identity for what we do. What do the people I meet at a wine fair or across a conference table see, and what would I like them to see? Paola in our communications office once joked that when I arrive in New York, I'm like Sophia Loren: I represent all the good things that foreigners associate with Italy, meaning elegance, creativity, good taste, *la dolce vita*. In reality, I don't think that's the case, but certainly when I go abroad I feel proud to be Florentine and to represent a city that is so beloved around the world.

Outside of Italy, an Italian businessman can't take on the burden of representing the entire country, especially a country that is so powerful in the collective international imagination. The same goes for Tuscany, by which I mean Tuscany as an historic place and as a land admired for its style and Italian quintessence, but also the actual modern-day Tuscany with its earth, stones, and clay.

Albiera would choose a horseback ride in the vineyards over a fancy party any day, and she likes to say that the Antinoris are still grape growers, people who work the soil and get their hands dirty. Since the moment when my father understood that wine must provide pleasure and not just quench thirst, we have not acquired grapes elsewhere and then used them to make wine in our cellars. We follow the process from the planting of the vines to the moment the bottles are carefully laid on the shelves of a wine store. "Great wine is born of great vineyards," Giacomo Tachis is fond of repeating. "Farmers make the best wine," Luigi Veronelli used to say. The Tuscan countryside is a concrete symbol of our history. We can travel the world with our heads held high, planting new vineyards on every continent, because our roots are so strong in Bolgheri and Tignanello, in Badia a Passignano and Montalcino.

I should say something here about titles. They're useful mostly for public relations. In Florence, with my colleagues and in the newspapers, I'm known as Marchese Antinori, but we're still a family of salespeople from the Florentine Republic, if a particularly enduring family. Over the centuries, Antinoris have gone everywhere, and they've flourished everywhere, from Argentina to Southern Italy. Our own archives and various books and essays written about my family indicate that we have always been more concerned with substance than with celebrity or high society.

That's the case today, too. We're part of the world of ancient noble Florentine families, with its rituals and connections, but you're likely to find us among the rows of Sangiovese grapes or out with our dogs or our horses. We see ourselves as merchants, proud of our wares and our work.

Then there are the titles that are not inherited, but earned through hard work. The British magazine *Decanter* named me Man of the Year in 1986. I was the first Italian to receive that honor, and then in 2011 the magazine also named me the most powerful man in Italian wine. I received the Premio Leonardo Qualità Italia from the president of Italy in 2004, was named best producer at Vinitaly 2006 and received a Lifetime Achievement Award from *Wine Enthusiast* in 2008, among many other honors. My company's visibility and my commitment to my country, my region, and to the world of wine earned me the presidency of Federvini and membership in the Accademia Italiana della Vite e del Vino. Like several of my ancestors, I'm part of the Accademia dei Georgofili. Today I'm president of the Istituto del Vino di Qualità Grandi Marchi. But if I had to choose the greatest honor I've received, it would have to be when Italian president Oscar Luigi Scalfaro made me a Cavaliere del Lavoro in 1995. My father was similarly honored in 1952 by Luigi Einaudi for both his winemaking success and the changes he was bringing to the countryside in and around Bolgheri. Our certificates hang near each other on a wall of the boardroom in Palazzo Antinori. However, my father's favorite title was less formally bestowed: he loved it when his friends referred to him simply as "the Vintner."

That reminds me of someone I met during my early days, Lino DeVito. He was addressed as *Marchese*, but I could never confirm whether his family was officially titled. No matter: his commitment and generosity were certainly noble.

Born in Abruzzo in the 1920s, De Vito had had an active youth and had been with a lot of women. At some point, he began to find the attention paid to him by all these women—and maybe by some of their husbands—unwelcome, and he left for New York. There, to make ends meet, he hit the sidewalks of Manhattan, selling wine for a small Italian-American company. He continued to do that for the rest of his life, until he passed away a few years ago. He took sales—at the time considered a rather undignified job—and made it into an art.

When he arrived in the United States, Italian wines were found on the tables of poor-quality restaurants with immigrant customers, the kind of places with spaghetti and meatballs, veal piccata, and spumoni on the menu. These things were unknown to Italians in Italy, but they had somehow come to be seen as classics. In other words, Italian food was not exactly considered haute cuisine at the time. De Vito struck a real coup when he managed to get Soave Bolla on the wine list of the Colony, New York's most chic boîte in those days. The Colony was owned by a man of Italian descent, a New Yorker named Gene Cavallero, but it was no humble trattoria. It was a classy place frequented by politicians, movie stars, and billionaires.

De Vito is said to have used the influence of an acquaintance of his, the daughter of a New York tycoon. However he managed it, getting in with the Colony was like receiving a key to the city. He'd conquered America, and in doing so he laid the groundwork for those of us who came after him.

When I started working in the Big Apple with him, I kept hearing people call out *"Marchese!"* and I'd turn around, thinking they were talking to me. But I was wrong: he was the "Italian wine marquis" in this city. He put so much dignity and passion into selling wine that he made it seem like the most important work in the world. In New York, De Vito would enter an exclusive restaurant as if he were an important guest they'd been expecting. He knew everyone and knew everything about them, and they all loved him. He was always ready to lend a hand or give some advice, but he could quickly shut down anyone who tried to take advantage of him. Working with him and watching his style and passion in the years he worked with us taught me so much. My title may be more authentic, but he displayed true nobility—wine nobility.

In the end, that is what it is all about for me; I'd much rather talk about our work and our wines than about myself, and the same is true of my daughters. As dedicated as we are to being the public face of this family business, we remain very private people. Palazzo Antinori is always open to tourists, coworkers, and the Florentine sunshine, but there is a staircase that goes from the courtyard up to our residence on the upper floors. The area up there is our private space, out of the public eye. Everyone needs that.

Our home represents us well. It's a stone refuge planted on Tuscan soil, a few meters from the Arno River, topped with a family crest made in 1512 by the della Robbia family, the renowned Renaissance ceramic artists. For five centuries Palazzo Antinori has been our headquarters and our family home. It has its own story, and that story starts with a woman.

Camilla Marsuppini was a Florentine beauty in the fifteenth century. There's a small portrait of her on the frieze of a chimney-piece sculpted by Desiderio da Settignano that today is housed in the Victoria and Albert Museum in London. Her hand was given in marriage to Giovanni, the son of wealthy Florentine banker and silk merchant Bono di Giovanni di Bartolo Boni. Camilla was the subject of a lot of gossip. It's not entirely clear what happened—a relationship ended badly or she offended someone she shouldn't have—but her husband asked for a separation. This was unheard of at the time and was a disgrace for Camilla and her family. The Marsuppinis decided to avenge themselves, and Giovanni was killed by a brother-in-law.

What does that have to do with us? Shortly before his death, the banker had purchased a large and desirable piece of land in front of the small church of San Michele Bertelde (today known as Santi Michele e Gaetano) and just a few steps from the Arno and the Baptistery for his son and his bride. The medieval houses that had been located there were razed and a large building was being built as a tangible and unmistakable sign of the status and power of the Boni family. Because of the family feud Camilla caused, the plans went bust. A dead son, a disowned daughter-in-law, a stain on all their children, consequent economic ruin, and a loss of face for everyone involved. In 1470, the Bonis went bankrupt and their land—an expensive construction site smack in the middle of Florence—became a burden and a reminder of unhappy times, and they wanted to be rid of it as soon as possible.

That set off some competition among well-off families for the ideally located property. The Medici family, lords of Florence, got involved and assigned it to the Martelli family. A few years later, in February 1506, the large stone building passed to the family that would own it for ages: on the advice of Lorenzo il Magnifico, Niccolò di Tommaso Antinori purchased it from the Martellis for 4,000 florins. Ever since, it's been our main home, our symbol, and our headquarters. Niccolò bought it as a way to confirm the success the Antinoris had achieved in banking and textiles. Soon after, though, it became what it remains—a sanctuary for my family and an important address.

Today, we are an integral part of Florence. There is a narrow Via Antinori that leads to the house, and the square where the house is located is now known as Piazza Antinori. On the other side, next to the Santi Michele e Gaetano church, the Antinori Chapel, built in the early seventeenth century by Bastiano, Lorenzo, and Vincenzio Antinori, still stands. It contains the tomb of Alessandro Antinori and was beautifully restored by my father. It is closed to the public, and we all use it as a spot for quiet reflection.

My father loved to tell a story about the palazzo that was also contained in the local history books. I found an old photocopy of it tucked among the photographs in one of his albums. At the dawn of the Renaissance, a group of friends gathered around a table on the loggia—today partly covered—to celebrate the arrival of summer. The group included priests from the city and the surrounding area, among them parish priest Pievano Arlotto.

Arlotto was a real person in Florence in the early 1400s, but his name has become a kind of shorthand for a priest who likes to have a good time. In paintings, stories, and jokes, he's depicted as a lover of good food and drink, as well as jokes and pranks. (Even after his death, Arlotto continued to joke around. His tomb in the Gesù Pellegrino oratory reads, "Pievano Arlotto had this tomb made for himself and anyone else who wants to come in.") Halfway through dinner, the group ran out of wine. Usually the servants delivered wine by tying the bottles to a loop of rope that they ran through the center of a spiral staircase that no longer exists. That evening, however, the servants weren't there. One of the guests would have to go down and get wine from the barrels.

The others conspired to convince Arlotto to go, and he did, albeit reluctantly. He liked to have a good time, but he didn't like to work much. He went down, poured wine, and returned, huffing and puffing. But the famously good-humored man looked concerned.

"What's wrong?" his host asked.

"I'm not sure that I remembered to close the barrels!" he answered.

In a flash, the entire group left their glasses and plates behind and ran down the stairs to check whether the cellar was flooded with precious red wine. Arlotto had tricked them all!

That happened right here, where I'm writing this now.

In order to understand how important this place is to us, you need to know about the short period when the stone facade with its asymmetrical wooden door did not belong to the Antinoris.

The 1920s were not happy times. In order to cut back on maintenance expenses and because they needed funds, my relatives decided to sell Palazzo Antinori. (I should note that this was not my direct branch of the family, but another, nonwinemaking branch that has since come to an end.) The division was created under the famous Vincenzio, the senator-cum-scientist who had two sons: Giuseppe Niccolò and Niccolò Giuseppe (fortunately we've always been more creative with the names of our wines than we are with the names of our children). Giuseppe Niccolò, born in 1844 and three years older than his brother, was chosen to carry on the family name. And his grandchildren let the building go.

Once the building had been sold, it first served as the offices for a small Tuscan bank (its name now forgotten) and then for the

Banca Nazionale del Lavoro, a major Italian bank. My side of the Antinori family lived then in the Palazzo Capponi on Via Gino Capponi. They rented the house, but they considered it their own, though they spent a great deal of time in their vineyards in the country. My father lived there, and my aunts were born there. I remember that when a descendant of the Capponi family, Folco Farinola, announced that he planned to sell the house to the Municipality of Florence to be used as a school, my family panicked. Then, our benefactor and relative, Egisto Fabbri, decided to purchase Palazzo Capponi with funds from the sale of his Cézanne works. Basically, we thought we'd live there forever.

Another twenty years went by. My father was trying to relaunch our wines after the war, and we were literally picking up the pieces of the San Casciano cellars. My father decided that the family—we were the most direct Antinori descendants in Florence—should return to its true home, the place he would stand outside and look at on his walks down Via Tornabuoni. He sold Villa Antinori (which was no longer fit to inhabit) to do it. He made so many sacrifices, not to mention an enormous investment. In 1957, we moved back. During our long history, we'd really spent only a short time not living here—fewer than forty years in five centuries. Coming back in the twentieth century was a real triumph.

With love and passion, my father recreated the original furnishings in the rooms of the house. He had mementoes brought from our other homes: photos, paintings, ceramics, books, archives, his infantryman's helmet, Giovanni Vettorio Soderini's treatise on enology from 1610 with Bastiano Antinori's notes on it, the tiny stone hare that my grandfather gave to him on their first hunting trip together. We reestablished the offices on the ground floor and our residence above, overlooking the roofs of Florence. In the living room I keep a photo of myself with my mother in the same room standing in front of a tapestry of battle scenes. It was taken on the day we returned, and in it we're glowing with happiness. My father's move was heroic, guided by emotion but also by awareness that the building was an important symbol for both our family and our company. This combination home and office in the center of the city connects modern-day Antinoris with our past and our history.

The palace is miraculously intact in the heart of a city that has seen numerous rounds of rebuilding, assault, brutal bombing in 1943, and a disastrous flood in 1966. It is a tangible symbol of our passion for what we do and who we are, the headquarters of the style and strategy we try to implement as a family and a winemaking company. Much of what we do can be reduced to this: innovate always with an eye to quality, but keep the structure and essence of our history strong. The palazzo is more than half a millennium old, but the ideas that have developed here are constantly made new. Its door is always open to Florentines and foreigners, and it provides space for exhibits, conventions, tastings, and other events.

The history of Tuscan wine in the last half century can be found here, in the modern spirit built atop an ancient history of grapes. Chianti Classico was growing sour—both metaphorically and literally—in the very years when quality, lightness, and elegance had come to the fore. A plan to improve it was conceived at Palazzo Antinori. We would open up our cellars to new techniques and new wine philosophies. This wasn't turning over a new leaf; it was recovering the essence of Chianti, using new tools and new knowledge to chip away at bad enological, commercial, and agricultural habits that had formed around it. (We'll get back to this eventually.)

Albiera, Allegra, and Alessia work in the building, too, though they've chosen not to live there with their families. We hatch plans over shared breakfasts and during our daily meetings around the large table in the office on the ground floor, among the old prints, various degrees, and the wines that look down on us from the shelves—with visitors in the Cantinetta Antinori across the hall and the sound of scooters buzzing up Via Tornabuoni coming in through the window. More and more I don't need to attend these meetings, and leave the members of the twenty-sixth generation of the family to make key decisions, often over glasses of wine.

Again, family is key to our style. The magic formula. A delicate alchemy that helps us combine life and work, because in many ways they are the same for us. All of this—family, the passing along of an idea, the pleasure of doing things well and always improving, my connection to my region and its culture and to my home—all of this is transmitted into the wines. It shows in every gesture and word that I use. The wine is born of my native land. It ages and improves based on my knowledge and experience; it is the thing I do best and that most represents me. Add meticulous attention to detail, the quest for the utmost quality, and a willingness to learn and grow. I believe that's true for my daughters and our colleagues as well.

You're probably starting to get the message. The legacy and continuity that we are selling, my signature on the label, our roots: these things mean that even when times are tough, I wouldn't dream of letting the company out of our control. Family history can't simply be sold off, especially because any buyer would do things differently than we do them.

I want to know at all times how our name is being used and where that label is going—on a bottle of wine or a dish of *pappa al pomodoro.*

Otherwise it won't work. Not at all.

4

TIGNANELLO

Reinventing Wine

*T*he 1975 vintage is the perfect Tignanello. People fall in love with it at first taste. As you open it, smell it, and taste it, luminous and pure aromas alternate with each other— spices, wet hay, and tobacco. It offers an intense and long-lasting structure with a vibrant and sweet finish. Honestly, making intense, flavorful wines under the Italian sun isn't difficult. The challenge is to make them so elegant that they don't need to shout to get attention. In our culture, it's common to measure a bottle's importance based on the percentage of alcohol it contains, which doesn't encourage the crafting of that type of wine.

I feel especially proprietary about the 1975 Tignanello. The wine that came out of that harvest and those bottles was exactly what I wanted and imagined it could be. A vineyard and an idea: that's the essence of an important wine. Sheer will, applied to the right vines and the right terroir—that magical French word that indicates specific soil and a specific environment that will give the wine its character; collaboration with those you esteem and trust, sticking to a plan in the face of natural and cultural obstacles.

I like to think that in each of those new wines born in Tuscany in the 1960s and 1970s there is a little bit of the personality of each person who helped to create them—the faces, gestures, ideas, and words encountered along the sometimes rocky road that led to Solaia and especially to Tignanello. Without them, our vineyards would offer nothing more interesting than a good Chianti. That kind of wine has its place—accompanying a nice thick Florentine steak, for example—but it doesn't win international prizes. Enologists don't fight for it, and it will never be deemed an important wine in Italian winemaking history. My life and Tuscan vineyards would be completely different without those people.

When I took over the company, Giacomo Tachis had been our enologist for five years. We became friends immediately and held each other in high esteem. We found we were on the same page when it came to wine, and that's still true. Tachis had the same kind of relationship with my father. He liked Niccolò as a man and as a vintner, and once wrote that my father was born with "great wine chromosomes." My father described Tachis as "intelligent and passionate" and a major supporter of the kind of enology that was turning winemaking into a science. He was eternally grateful to Tachis for safeguarding and improving his beloved sparkling wines over the years.

Tachis began his career with a company in Romagna that would make anything anyone ordered: vermouth, liqueur, wine, and so on. All the customer had to do was pay for it. Their products may not have won any prizes, but they provided excellent training for Tachis. He earned a reputation for being quick, hardworking, and capable of thinking on his feet. And then a bit of luck brought him to Antinori.

For some time my father had been grooming Checcucci, the young man he thought would be the company's next enologist. He was a nice guy, and my father had funded his education at the Scuola Enologica in Conegliano Veneto, where he'd recently earned an enology degree. Unfortunately, when he started working in the field with real-world deadlines and expectations, there were issues. He couldn't perform under pressure and he had trouble applying theory in concrete form. He also didn't relate well to his colleagues. He just wasn't the right fit. What Vittorio Alfieri termed the "human plant" can grow in unpredictable ways.

Piergiovanni Garoglio suggested that my father hire Tachis to fill the position. This was a ringing endorsement. Garoglio was the top Italian professor of enology and agriculture at the time. He was quirky and moody—almost a caricature of an academic—and his writing on the chemistry of wine was seminal. (Though it pains me to say so, the work is a little dated now.) He'd traveled and studied in Germany and Argentina. When he returned to Florence after the war, he worked with us and was a frequent presence in our home. Once, in the 1940s, when I was still practically a child, he pushed me to make my first demijohn of wine using some grapes from the Tignanello vineyard in Santa Cristina, and he came by often to see how I was doing with it. (Like Albiera and Allegra, I had my own "toy wine.")

Tachis soon became indispensable. He provides yet another example of how the successes I've achieved are built on ideas and choices made by my father, beginning with the fact that wine's evolution, from mere fuel for working in the fields to a substance that provides an emotional experience, is inspired by a team of colleagues who were practiced professionals and wonderful human beings, all sharing the same kind of drive.

My first enologist was born in 1933 in Poirino, south of Turin, an ancient seat of the House of Savoy that is famous for many things—asparagus, the stench of its canals, its wild Carnevale celebrations—but not for wine. Like all great Piedmontese winemakers, he studied in Alba, capital of the Langhe area, but Tuscany is his second home and the place where he learned most of what he knows and achieved his greatest results. Tachis is a natural talent with a deep and wide-ranging passion for wine. In addition to creating, promoting, and studying it, he's also a bibliophile who for many years has immersed himself in all cultural expressions involving the "nectar of the gods," including poetry, art, and religious symbolism.

A short time ago he decided to retire, to the dismay of the entire Italian wine world. He was the creative mind in the group that had formed around me during my apprenticeship as director. I spoke about that over bottles of 1982 Tignanello and 2001 Cervaro della Sala at a very special dinner in spring 2011, at which Giacomo was officially named Man of the Year by *Decanter*.

He was recognized before an audience of winemakers and friends who have been lucky enough to work with him everywhere from Tuscany to Sardinia. The crystal decanter that Tachis received was an acknowledgment of lifetime achievement in the world of wine and his impact behind the scenes of the renaissance in Italian wines. "Making even one great wine is a high achievement, and making more than one is extraordinary," said *Decanter* editor Sarah

Kemp, "but it's truly exceptional to have made so many that are of such high quality and to have contributed to raising the bar for the entire country, from Maremma to the islands."

She's right. Tachis not only gave the world some wonderful wines and introduced certain techniques for varietals and fermentation in Italy (he's especially well-known for malolactic fermentation), but he truly created a new philosophy of wine, establishing once and for all that wine reflects the land where it is created. It is the distilled essence of that land. He taught us that making high-quality wine in a certain valley, on a certain hill, in a certain countryside means helping that place express itself—drawing out its soul. And that soul can then be bottled and travel the world, where it will speak of that place and its people.

I'd known Giovanni Santoni, our longtime sales director and another member of our team, for a long time. I'd always seen him as a kind of marketing psychologist more than anything else—a man who didn't have a formal education in economics but had an instinct about people and the precious gift of being a good judge of character and of the expectations of salespeople and customers. If he was the brains behind the sales operations, Giancarlo Notari, his mentee and close colleague, was the soul of the operation. He'd been a friend forever. We're the same age, and we began to work in the palazzo in Florence on the same day. He was an ambassador for Antinori. When he retired in 1997 to dedicate himself to the wines of the Compagnia del Vino, he had worked with me for thirty-one years, demonstrating great love for our wines and our company.

This team changed Tuscan wine. We were all afflicted with "acute Antinoritis," as the great Piedmontese winemaker Angelo Gaja recently called it during an evening honoring Giacomo Tachis.

We are wine people, united by a strong passion. We were from different backgrounds, but our days, our formative experiences, and maybe even our memories and our worlds had always been the same.

So we had a team. But what challenges were we up against?

To understand how Tignanello came to be, we should start with what rural Tuscany was like when I began running the company. Those were the years when owners were beginning to work their fields and vineyards directly rather than using the ancient *mezzadria,* or sharecropping system. One era was drawing to an end, and another was beginning—somewhat chaotically. *Mezzadria* had been the norm throughout central Italy for centuries, beginning in the late Middle Ages. A house made of plaster and stone up on a hill, a row of cypress trees, and a barn. Small towns gathered around a church amid the fields and gardens where cauliflower and beans grew. These are the symbols of Tuscany, and they all developed due to that system.

This is how it worked: I, the owner, allowed you, the farmer, to live on my land in the farmhouse with your family and tend the fields and raise animals. You could pass along that position to your children and their children and so on. In return, half (or a smaller percentage established by law) of what you grew and the profits you made were handed over to me. This common practice filled the Italian countryside with solid farmhouses where generations of sharecroppers, under the guidance of their patriarchs, worked the fields that belonged to bosses who often lived far away and frequently evinced little interest in the property, so long as they got their due share.

The farmers were basically left to manage on their own. In order to produce more on the land and be self-sufficient, they grew crops in the fields and the vineyards, but also in the orchards and olive groves. They tended kitchen gardens and raised chickens, pigs, cows, and rabbits. Grapes were grown amid the trees and other crops. Countryside, nature, and the seasons were in balance. It was a closed ecosystem that seemed like it would last forever, but at a closer glance, it was revealed to be a system that took advantage of and weakened the farmers. Neither party had any interest in improving techniques, investing in experiments or research, or redefining roles and responsibilities. The Tuscany of that era was harmonious and poetic, but it was frozen in time like a postcard.

Today, there are few traces left of that period. They exist more in the mental landscape than in reality. Now, high-quality producers use their own grapes, which are for the most part grown using certified processes. When I was a kid, using your own grapes meant you could only make enough wine for your own home use. The few large-scale producers around had to look elsewhere for grapes.

Since the time of Boccaccio and Petrarch, there were middlemen in Tuscany who went from farm to farm, from family to family, helping to bring supply and demand together (for a 2 percent commission), or buying and selling lots of grapes, as well as oil, corn, hay, straw, and chickpeas. This was a highly specialized line of work that was passed down through generations, so that a family name would serve as a guarantee of the quality of the items. It required experience and charisma. Brokers of this type were colorful people, often very well dressed, who made the rounds in horse-drawn carriages full of samples. In winter, they often sported showy orange overcoats with fox-fur collars. The one I remember best from my own childhood was a guy named Matteuzzi who worked in San Casciano and was known as Ciapo. (Back then, every single person in a small town was given a nickname that stuck to him his whole life.) An indefatigable visitor to the Chianti farms, trustworthy and a great storyteller, Ciapo then had a son who—of course—also became a middleman and—again, of course—was known to everyone as Ciapino, or little Ciapo. Both of them worked with us for a long time.

Overseers were also crucial at the time. The landowners—especially those noblemen who preferred to stay in the city or spend their time hunting—hired overseers to handle their land. This kind of work, too, was often passed down through the generations, which meant that they learned the techniques and knowledge of the vineyard (and how to "round up" their pay) from their fathers and grandfathers. These traditions in their revised and more appropriate form are still part of modern winemaking, and key to ensuring that the ongoing struggle between globalization and maintaining high quality does not eradicate identity and a sense of origins. Family relations—as the history of my own family demonstrates—are a conduit for passing down knowledge. They can inspire customer loyalty and faith in a known brand. This was true one hundred years ago and it's true today: our current administrative director, Fabrizio Panattoni, is the son of Idalgo, who was the overseer first in Bolgheri and later in Castello della Sala. Many of the workers in our vineyards and cellars are the children and grandchildren of people who did the same kind of work for us at one time. And even those who were not directly involved in the *mezzadria* system were part of it. The attention and energy of an entire community was long focused on the cellars in San Casciano.

They weren't our farmers and they weren't members of a family that farmed in the area, but I will never forget the Matteuzzi family (the same name as our grape middleman). Giancarlo Matteuzzi, who was twelve at the time and later became a schoolteacher, recalls that during the tragic days of the German retreat, all the families tried to hide what little they had from the raiding soldiers. They hid the men in the family, too, because the Germans would take them away to dig holes for planting mines. With disaster looming, some of the company's employees decided to save a large number of valuable bottles. But where to hide them? They safely stored them in a large, empty cistern in the courtyard of the Matteuzzi home. It was risky, but the family didn't hesitate to protect this small treasure. The wine was perceived as belonging to the entire town. The cistern was closed up tightly with old boards.

The Germans passed through that very spot and conducted a search. They marched right over the boards on top of the cistern, but they didn't realize there was anything underneath. "I'll always remember the pounding of their boots as they walked right above that hidden wine," said Giancarlo. The people who had saved our bottles returned them to us intact. That's just one example of one family who defended the estate and the warehouses; they were not the only ones. We still exist because of those people and their attachment to the company.

Our cellar master from that time also taught me a lesson about affection for the product. His name was Checcucci, and his family had been in San Casciano for ages. (He was the father of the Checcucci who went to enology school and briefly served as the Antinori enologist.) He was known as Lallo. Brilliant and eccentric, he worked for Antinori his entire life and was very proud to do so.

Naturally, he liked to drink. He was weaned, raised, and aged on Chianti. At that time it was a normal thing to drink the same wine your entire life—the wine of your land, your city. It might even have been the wine your own family produced for personal use. You had that wine in your veins. Once my father gave him a taste of a very rare Château Lafite, the king of Bordeaux wines. This is a very elegant wine, with hints of cedar, a red that in recent years has garnered astronomical prices at auction, making it the most expensive wine of all time. Lallo took just one sip, spat it onto the ground, and protested with disdain, "That's not wine!"

The end of these Chianti "vignettes" came by law. In September 1964, the Italian government abolished the signing of any new *mezzadria* contracts and announced that any already underway would soon end. This move was meant to put a stop to what was seen by many as a feudal system and to create a farming boom in Italy, as well as to modernize the field of agriculture. Many farmers couldn't find positions in this new rural economy or became regular employees and moved to nearby towns. Traveling our highways today, you can still see a lot of run-down, abandoned farmhouses out in the country. The fields were emptied, and in an attempt to turn a profit and cover new expenses derived from direct management of those fields, too many landowners began trying to grow grapes.

Millions of grapevines sprang up, covering every inch of land. What had been an area of judiciously planted small vineyards was quickly covered with swaths of light green, all growing the same crop. In other areas, thanks to European programs, land was chosen carefully for those early transitional years, yet here in the heart of ancient wine territory, grapes grew with little oversight. Many of the people growing them lacked even the most basic knowledge of what to do. Their motto seemed to be, "The wine made here has always been good. Let's plant as much as possible and see what happens."

Vineyards were planted in wholly unsuitable places: at the bottom of valleys, on hillsides with poor exposure. Compare that prizing of quantity over quality to today, when "cloning" is used to select and prepare plants from the time they are in the nursery. Quality demands the best of the best. Back then, nursery owners provided shoots to people who had suddenly become grape growers, and since they were faced with overwhelming demand out of nowhere, they scraped the bottom of the barrel and offered anything they could find, including unpedigreed Sangiovese plants. It was a disaster, and some signs of that disaster can still be seen today, because a vineyard that's planted poorly will continue to punish you for a long time.

The first consequence of all this was the loss of a landscape. To make room for these large vineyards, bulldozers were brought in to dig up wonderful terraces and knock down old stone walls. Vegetable gardens and orchards were destroyed. Rows were planted farther apart in order to make room for large machines to trundle between them. Things moved quickly, and there was a big push to see earnings from the investments being made. The actual number of vines per hectare was small, but those vines were forced to yield enormous numbers of grapes. High-quality Tuscan wine requires the exact opposite arrangement.

The whole system collapsed. Local and national governments barely lifted a finger to moderate and regulate. And when they did, they caused even more damage, as was the case with a protocol that dictated that in order to obtain European Community funds from the FEOGA, an agricultural organization, vines had to be supported by standardized cement poles: a solution as unnatural and counterproductive as it was ugly to look at. Today in Chianti, most of those "synthetic" poles have been replaced by new wooden stakes, but that took years and was expensive, and the old poles caused environmental damage.

The quality of wine declined. To be fair, Chianti had been declining for some time. Some of the tenets that we winemakers held dear had proven to be the ruin of Chianti. I won't get into all the technical, enological detail, but suffice it to say that the widespread belief that a high level of acidity was the basis for longevity in red wine became a real defect. Today we know that wine has good potential for aging if it is rich in tannins and polyphenols, both of which are often lacking in Tuscan grapes.

One of the first complaints about the export of Tuscan wine dates to 1653, when in London a certain Charles Longland lamented in an urgent letter that the casks of Chianti that were delivered to him after traveling for months were of "poor quality." All it took was a storm in the English Channel, a problem at customs, and our wines suffered seasickness. And so did the importer. Three centuries later, the problem had not been resolved completely. I should note that in the early twentieth century, conscientious producers like my grandfather did manage to sell abroad, even to South America. But in general, the situation was fraught—especially as it became fairly common practice to pass off as Chianti wines low-quality wines from other areas of Tuscany and made with other grapes. By the early twentieth century, despite the increasingly strict rules and prohibitions, it was almost impossible to say what was a Chianti wine.

In conclusion, unpedigreed Sangiovese grown in vineyards that were hurriedly thrown together in the post-*mezzadria* period meant that fifty years ago the autumn harvest yielded wine with few good tannins and high acidity that oxidized readily. Also, the climate was already beginning to change, even though we've only really begun to talk about that in recent years. There were long, hot summers and tropical temperatures. Weak raw material was examined in the most cursory manner and then aged in barrels that were the wrong size but were used to save money; they were made from poor-quality wood and reused for decades. In the end, the Chianti that went into the bottles was thin, watery, and lacking in body. It was born weak and tired and it could not age properly. As quality declined, the image of our labels and our land declined as well. Prices fell, and there was less demand for the wine to be exported. The end result was a crisis that hit the entire Tuscan countryside.

I began to see that we could only escape this vicious cycle by working in several areas at once. We would have to stand behind the moral imperative of the Antinoris: always improve and strive for the best possible quality. That's not some empty slogan. It was the only way in that diseased landscape to make things better, as it is in today's global crisis. If it's been a tough year, the worst thing you can do is to save what can be saved and then sit around and wait for better times to come. The first thing you should do is try something new—study, look around, clean out the old, and invest in the future. The alternative is to change your line of work, which is exactly what many wine producers did in the late 1960s.

The link between wine and its habitat needed to be reestablished, beginning with the magnificent land accumulated by my family over the years. At the same time, there was a need for a "wine reinvention," something that may not ever have been attempted in Tuscany. Finally, I tried to look at things as a consumer. We couldn't just turn back the clock on the disastrous 1960s and go back to making the wine of my grandfather and Pievano Arlotto. When I started to think about what would come to be known as the Super Tuscans, it was in part because even I no longer liked the best and most honest red wines of the day. When I sat down at the table and drank the wines I'd been drinking my entire life, I felt as if something was missing. I wanted something more refined, better structured, more recognizable, and with more personality.

The trail had been blazed by my father, who, often in conflict with my grandfather and the winemaking world of his time, came back from his travels full of ideas and focused on innovation. New blends, such as Cabernet mixed with Sangiovese (for the first time in 1924), new types of barrels, temperature control for fermentation and in the cellar: these were the stuff of science fiction at the time. Giacomo Tachis and I talked day and night. We felt there had to be something more. Thanks to him, in those exploratory years I looked to France for inspiration, just as my father had done. And I was lucky to meet Professor Émile Peynaud.

The meeting between the most influential Italian enologist of his time and the French genius who inspired modern Bordeaux has become legendary. As a student in Alba in the early 1950s, Tachis did not hesitate to write directly to the most famous experts when he had a question about yeast or fermentation. Peynaud sensed his intelligence and precocity and answered him right away, sending him some of his published work. That was that. But in 1968, my trusted enologist and I took one of our exploratory journeys to the French Bordeaux region. As Tachis recalls it, the purpose of that expedition was initially to meet another luminary, Professor Pascal Ribéreau-Gayon, author of major winemaking manuals, and invite him to act as consultant.

Upon arriving in France, we discovered that the great man was out of town for a conference. We set up some other meetings so that the trip wouldn't be a complete waste of time. I distinctly recall that a local friend of ours, the Baron de Luze, gave us a hand. The baron was a landowner and *négociant*, a word that still today in France indicates someone involved in the purchase and sale of wine. In France, unlike Italy, this was considered a very specialized and high-level job. In addition to letting us stay with him, de Luze advised us to contact the enology department at the University of Bordeaux directly for a consultation. At the time, it was the most famous such department in the world. That was where we met Tachis's long-time idol. Peynaud not only remembered his young correspondent from Piedmont, but was so taken with his passionate descriptions that he immediately accepted our invitation to visit the cellars in San Casciano. Shortly afterward, he began consulting for us.

Peynaud passed away in 2004 at the age of ninety-two. He was one of the few true giants of the wine world in the last half century. He was a prodigy who at fifteen worked for the Maison Calvet and at twenty published work in the *Revue de Viticulture*. His was a mind that not only made a profound impact on the new world of Tuscan wines, but had already revolutionized the cellars of France as well. He changed everything: selection of grapes, level of ripeness, acidity, casks, fermentation (he was the one who taught us all about malolactic fermentation).

Additionally, in my opinion he had the rare ability to marry extraordinary scientific knowledge with flexible, practical skill in the vineyards and the cellars. He was a scientist, a prestigious enology academic—many of his works are still valid and current—who refined his knowledge and theory by "getting his hands dirty" at many different types of wineries, from the best châteaux, to the traditional estates of Bordeaux, to vineyards in Italy and Greece. He was a brilliant writer with a great capacity to communicate and share information. He was always teaching and always transmitting his passion for wine, though he spoke only French. He was an intellectual with an earthy approach: Peynaud loved eating and drinking and trying new things. He was as happy to drink a great wine as he was to encounter an unknown and interesting label. I've never met anyone whose life revolved around wine the way his did—in the library, in the cellars, or at the table with friends. "Everyone drinks the wine that he deserves," he used to say. He also used to say, "Tradition is an experiment that was successful."

Thanks to his special relationship with Tachis and his appreciation of our attempts to relaunch high-quality Tuscan wines, Peynaud studied our grapes, saw the potential for my project, and made our cause his own. With his annual visits to Tuscany, between one dinner and the next in Tignanello or Castello della Sala, he helped us formulate a different philosophy for this new wine. That philosophy was basically a list of what *not* to do. Our French teacher said, "To obtain a high-quality red, you must not use large percentages of white grapes, which is common in your country. Nor can you close it up in oversized chestnut barrels for three or four years, or always use the same barrels." Basically, the usual formula for Chianti had to be turned upside down.

It was the so-called Iron Baron, Bettino Ricasoli, a great wine-maker and politician, who in the early twentieth century came up with the standard Chianti blend. This man, who was Italy's second head of government (successor to Camillo Benso, the Count of Cavour), determined that Chianti Classico should be based on Sangiovese. He also dictated that white grapes be added to "soften" the flavor of the wine, which, already tannic by nature, was even stronger and more astringent back then because there were no modern tools for destemming. Ricasoli also recommended Malvasia as the grape that would be best for "cutting" the wine. This variety was grown with great success in Tuscany until the fourteenth century (it seems to have been introduced just after the frightening plague of 1348, when the gardeners of Florence were trying out new techniques and grapes to reclaim the semiabandoned countryside).

Ricasoli's were carefully thought-out ideas. Despite the long crisis in our countryside that lasted until the end of the Medici era, many brilliant minds had begun to rethink the local wine, if slowly. In 1716, Cosimo III, grand duke of Tuscany, established the first geographic boundaries for high-quality Tuscan vineyards. And from 1753, our region was by far the most evolved in terms of agricultural science thanks to the founding of the Accademia dei Georgofili (with the participation of Vincenzio Antinori). That important association is still active today. It's run by Franco Scaramuzzi, a personal friend of mine and the former chancellor of the University of Florence, as well as an eminent expert in agriculture and a passionate farmer himself.

As the Lorena clan took the throne left vacant by the Medicis, a widespread plan for relaunching agriculture in the area was put in place in Florence. Finally, in 1895, the first prototype of the Chianti consortium was born. It had a commercial brand indicating origin. So, in light of the ideas of that time, the baron hit upon a good formula. Unfortunately, as time passed, in order to make increasingly imprecisely crafted Chianti drinkable and saleable, many people began to lose sight of its very essence, adding up to 30 percent white grapes, particularly Trebbiano grapes, as they were hardy and easy to grow, albeit not of great quality. In the late 1960s, our enemy was not the law as established by Ricasoli, but progressive decline, shortcuts taken by farmers and overseers in search of quick profit that had become common practice.

I had Peynaud's advice and Tachis's talent on my side. I had a team of workers who had been with me since I'd taken over from my father and taken Benazzi's place. And I also had the encouragement of a big name in Italian wine history: Luigi Veronelli, the journalist/enologist *par excellence* who was already one of Italy's strictest and most influential critics. I'd been reading his work forever, but I'd only recently met him in person.

Veronelli confirmed that my ideas were a step in the right direction. Yes, it was time for a new Chianti that would bring the sector back from the brink. Yes, it was okay to let the old rules go, to rely on "outside" grapes, and to change times and processes. And, yes, the base for the wine should be the best Chianti grapes, from vineyards whose products were certified and that we had known for centuries. Simultaneously, to the southeast a modest experiment had become an international sensation, and that, too, gave me the strength to go forward.

In the early 1940s, Mario Incisa della Rocchetta, from an old Piedmont family, famous raiser of horses, lover of French wines, and my uncle, noticed that the landscape around his San Guido estate on the Livorno coast near Bolgheri resembled the Graves area in Bordeaux. This part of Tuscany was completely different from our Chianti area—it was an untrammeled wild place with salty sea air. Just a few years earlier the swamps had been drained and the land had been saved from brigands and from malaria. We were familiar with it because we had a vacation home there on property owned by my mother, Carlotta della Gherardesca. Mario Incisa, too, had acquired his land through marriage—with Clarice della Gherardesca, my mother's sister.

My uncle was originally from Rocchetta Tanaro, the Asti-adjacent birthplace of Barbera wine, but he lived in Rome. Anything he did, he did well. He was also a partner of Federico Tesio, breeder of Ribot, one of the great horses of the 1950s. As the owner of this fine specimen of the Dormello Olgiata breed, he was in charge of the horse's final races. The French newspapers called Ribot "the best racecar ever seen on a racetrack."

The *marchese* was an environmentalist ahead of his time, and he decided that his land in the Maremma area should be protected. He was among the first to support creation of the Bolgheri "oasis." Once he had accepted the mission to protect the environment, he grew so committed that eventually he became president of the Italian World Wildlife Fund, formed in 1966, and then as now an important environmental organization. He had an open mind (not a common thing at the time) and could appreciate and understand the Tuscan countryside so far from his Piedmont plains. And he appreciated its vineyards and its wines as well. He was a true aesthete.

The della Gherardesca family had owned land in the area for centuries, and in the early nineteenth century one of them, Guido Alberto, attempted farming using modern tools and concepts picked up in France. He'd been the first to try to get a foreign variety known as Carmené—actually Cabernet—to take root along the coast of the Tyrrhenian Sea. In the next century, however, much of this work came undone during the years when the *mezzadria* system was dying a prolonged and painful death.

What did Mario Incisa do? He acquired enough Cabernet Sauvignon and Cabernet Franc plants from the Salvati dukes' Migliarino company to plant two vineyards. These were fantastic plants. It was said that the dukes themselves had gotten them from the celebrated Château Lafite vineyards in Bordeaux. Mario Incisa tended these plants very carefully. In 1944, he had already begun to bottle his "Maremma Bordeaux." As a country squire, for ten years my uncle produced wine only for his own use and for a small circle of friends, and he did so with little fanfare. "It's called Sassicaia. I make it in my garage," he would modestly explain.

That was in the mid-1960s, when the entire region was concentrating on "easy" Chianti. I'd admired my uncle and his wine for some time. More than once I'd accompanied him on a "field trip" to vineyards in France. So, in 1968 I suggested to him that he sell a few bottles of his wine, using our sales network. "Okay, but just a few," he agreed. I asked Tachis to work with him to make the Sassicaia a little less "homemade." We designed a label with the help of the old printer Pineider in Florence. Then we began to sell the wine.

We intended it almost as a lark, but it rocked the wine world. (Luigi Veronelli dedicated a paean to the wine from Bolgheri in the Italian magazine *Panorama*.) Not only was there an Antinori relative in Maremma who was making Cabernet, but his wine was high-quality and something completely new.

In the following ten years, Giacomo Tachis (who really only stopped handling this wine a couple of years ago) made Sassicaia one of Italy's most admired and influential wines. It transformed the town of Bolgheri into a winemaking Eden and rendered its cypress-lined roads and the landscape once lovingly described by native poet Giosuè Carducci a symbol of Tuscany. In 1974, *Decanter* magazine organized a "showdown" between traditional wines, and Sassicaia emerged with a higher rating than a slew of highly refined Bordeaux wines. A legend was born.

When my uncle passed away, my cousin Nicolò took over. I'd simply provided the initial impulse for that wave of creativity; I do remember, though, that someone interviewed me, convinced of the fact that Sassicaia was an Antinori invention. I was flattered, though I didn't hesitate to correct that misimpression and explain how things had really happened.

Everyone was talking about the San Guido wine. Now there was a model to follow. There was a plan. And when our old, glorious Villa Antinori from 1970 turned out to be vastly improved by the new processes used in the vineyards and the cellars that Peynaud had suggested and Tachis had implemented, we knew we should keep going. It was time to concentrate on the land. It was simple, really.

Where could a great wine be made if not on the estate where our best Sangiovese had always grown?

Today, the estate where we spent our vacations for a half century is home to the Tignanello and Solaia vineyards. My daughters and I have learned so much about grapes there. It's a place that was made for wine. Exposed to the sun from the southeast, three hundred fifty to four hundred fifty meters above sea level, with an incline and drainage that seem purposely engineered, Tignanello has the ideal rocky soil and the perfect climate. During the days, it's warm enough to develop sugars in the grapes, and at night the temperature cools to preserve the acids and develop the aroma. My father worked long and hard to plant the experimental Cabernet grapes here in the postwar period and then used them in his Villa Antinori. We were going to do things right and follow his example.

We produced only twenty thousand bottles of an early experimental Tignanello from the 1970 harvest. Created using new methods for selecting and handling grapes, it was a Chianti Classico with Sangiovese grapes and small amounts of white grapes. An excellent Chianti Classico, I must say, but still a traditional one in many ways. We labeled it "Villa Antinori" and then added "Tignanello Vineyard" next to that to be more exact.

The next year we cut our ties with the past completely. We finally crafted a mix free of white grapes. We harvested fully mature grapes. We fermented them with repeated repassing, a technique that consists of pouring the underlying liquid over the cap formed by the skins in order to extract the greatest amount of noble tannins from them. After alcoholic fermentation, the wine was subject to malolactic fermentation under the guidance of Peynaud.

This second type of fermentation creates better conditions for the malic acid in the grapes to generate lactic acid through the activity of certain bacteria. Without getting into too much technical detail, this is a natural process that solves the old problem of elevated acidity in our traditional grape mixtures, resulting in more balanced wines that age beautifully. Then it was time to let it sleep in small 225-liter barrels of new oak for a couple of years. These were the famous barriques that Luigi Veronelli would later rename *carati* in Italian during one of his visits to Tignanello. *Caratelli* were the small barrels traditionally used in Tuscany for aging vin santo, so the term was appropriate. Once the wine was out of the *carati,* it would age in bottles for another year.

Basically, we created something that was more Tuscan than its peers at the time and simultaneously completely new. In Tuscany, legend has it that at night Baron Bettino Ricasoli's ghost roams the woods around his family's home, the Brolio Castle, with a pack of hunting dogs. Perhaps on one of those nights, the winemaker's ghost visited our cellars, where we were changing his Chianti.

That was just the start of the revolution, however. Already there were plans to complete the "sacrilege" by adding to the Sangiovese the Cabernet that had made Sassicaia so unique and that my father had already used successfully. A few lesser harvests followed, however, when we stuck to the standard we had set for ourselves and didn't bottle any wine. In 1974, for the first time the Tignanello could come out of hiding to be tasted and evaluated, though it still didn't have a name or a label. Doubt began to cast a shadow.

To understand this moment, you have to know that in 1967 the DOC designation for Chianti had been introduced in Tuscany. This was a valid attempt to shut down the ubiquitous Chianti of dubious origin that had infested the global market. There was clearly an attempt to regulate the sector and separate the true Tuscan wine from the counterfeit, and to protect the health of consumers from foods that were not adequately monitored, in order to link an excellent product to the land it came from. What happened, though, was that many producers fooled themselves into thinking that this innovation would automatically lead to commercial success. There was a race to obtain DOC designation just for the sake of DOC designation that was unconvincing to me.

The philosophy behind this type of certification, which is increasingly common today and has been granted to very niche and very large-scale food and wine products alike in Italy, is necessary in the age of globalization and industrialization. In many ways, though, this system was intended to become the bible of Tuscan winemakers overnight, and instead it encountered an entrenched and conservative spirit. These regulations dictated what a Chianti was: How it tasted, what color it was, and how dark it was. How it could and could not be made. Basically, it established a method just when that method was growing outdated, and it left no room for experimentation or personal initiative.

It soon became clear that the new rules for DOC certification and my Tignanello spoke two different languages. There was no mention of abolishing white grapes, nor of authorizing the non-autochthonous (or nonindigenous) grapes that we were about to start using. The upshot of the story is that one of the most ambitious wines the company has made in six hundred years, a wine that was born in the heart of Tuscany, was not going to bear the words "Chianti Classico." What was a non-DOC wine in Italy? A table wine. The punishment for our sin of rebellion was that our bottles would appear to be fit only for the company cafeteria.

The price was also a problem. From dozens of generations of Antinoris, I had learned that we needed to improve in order to grow, and we needed to invest in order to improve. And I had invested: the cellars were completely new, there were new containers for each new type of fermentation, plus the expense of thousands of new barrels ordered from France at a high price. And much, much more. In order for it all to make sense, a bottle of Tignanello had to cost at least three times the going rate for a regular Chianti at the time. Should we ask our consumers to pay that extra amount for a Val di Pesa table wine? Marketing experts would have torn out their hair.

Basically, it was a dilemma of historic proportions. Until a few decades earlier, a bottle of wine cost less than double the price of a bottle of water. This margin certainly didn't inspire farmers to invest and improve. Progress had to be made by repositioning wine itself in the public imagination. That could only happen with a clear step forward in quality that would justify new value, a new price and, as a result, higher margins and new investments. So quality needed to be certified with DOC designations and other similar tools.

The problem from my point of view was that the legislation was diametrically opposed: mediocrity was being certified. I again spent sleepless nights in Palazzo Antinori. Fortunately, in those critical days in 1974, I had the support of my father and my team. Even Luigi Veronelli encouraged me; by then he had become the guardian angel for the whole project.

As I've mentioned already, Veronelli and I had met several times, and we had great respect for each other. But the star of new Italian winemaking knew nothing and suspected nothing about the complex "birth" of Tignanello. At the time he was in Orvieto at one of the first conferences—maybe even the first one ever—of the then-new Italian Sommelier Association. This was a small but historical event because it indicated progress in professional enology and a more serious consideration of the quality and culture of wine. From Castello della Sala, just a few minutes' drive away, I was following the work that these opinion leaders were doing. And one evening I managed to grab Veronelli for a few hours.

I brought him to dinner at the castle. He was served an excellent dish of pigeon with onions. I poured him a glass of that fateful 1971 wine without telling him what it was, and I watched his reaction. I saw his eyes light up with interest. "This is exceptional," he said. "What is it?" I told him. That evening, in the company of myself and Giovanni Santoni, the leading wine writer in Italy promised me that if I could produce a wine at that level of quality, the question of lack of DOC certification would be quickly forgotten. In the medieval rooms of the castle that had once belonged to the powerful Monaldeschi della Vipera family, he also gave me the name for that wine, noting that the simplest choice was the way to go: Tignanello. He explained, "The best thing you can do is to link this wine directly to its vineyard, its terroir, without embellishment. That will be its 'certification.'"

We gave our new creature an ancient name. It seems to have derived from the name of a family that lived in the spot long ago, the Tignani family. Marketing experts wouldn't have approved of the choice: the -ello suffix is a diminutive in Italian, making it sound like something insignificant. "Minor details!" Veronelli insisted. Besides, we cared more about that sense of belonging and historical identity. During that same dinner, Veronelli recommended a designer to create the label: Silvio Coppola, a standout graphic designer and artist already famous for his smooth and linear tables and lights.

He came up with an understated design with a large space for descriptive text, with few symbols and little color. Conceptual art was the style closest in spirit to the new generation of wines, after all. Even the label was innovative. And one small detail told a story: a single initial in black on the lower right. It wasn't my usual large P, a sail filled with wind and heading to the northeast. Instead, it was a small N, the signature of Niccolò Antinori.

I should explain why the wine that was most important to me and most closely linked to me personally bears the signature of my father. A few years earlier, Villa Antinori had been sold in the United States in a new package. In order to personalize our product further, our importers asked me as CEO to affix my signature to the label. I did it without giving it too much thought. It was a mistake. A Florentine friend came back from a trip to New York and reported back to my father, "You're being forced out of your own wine!" he said. My father let me know he wasn't happy. So having his signature on "my" wine wasn't an affectation; it was a way to make up for my mistake. And it wasn't the only thing that made Tignanello important to me.

After Veronelli met with me, he returned to Orvieto and organized the first tasting of Tignanello for a group of prestigious critics at the conference. It was a huge success. We had gotten the ball rolling. Tignanello had a name, a look, and a fast-growing reputation. That inspired us to create the second, "definitive" Tignanello vintage in 1975. The Sangiovese was perfect, and so was the Cabernet. It wasn't an indigenous grape, but it had been grown in our vineyards for many years. A small percentage of it in the blend gave my wine that touch of elegance and complexity that it had been missing.

We made twenty-five thousand unforgettable bottles. They were welcomed enthusiastically by critics and the public at large. In 1977, Veronelli was, naturally, the first to write about it, setting off demand in Italy and abroad. There were still those in the wine field who turned up their noses, of course. There was one who said Tignanello "fell outside of the tradition," and another who disdained the idea of aging in barrels.

I recall a Tignanello tasting where I feared the disapproval of Lamberto Paronetto, known as the "wine doctor." This very influential and serious man was the author of *Il Magnifico Chianti*, editor of *L'Enotecnico* magazine, a prize-winning master of the Office International de la Vigne et du Vin in Paris, and the recipient of many other accolades. If he were to simply raise an eyebrow in the right direction, it would mean everything for Antinori. At the fateful moment, Paronetto raised his glass, sniffed gently, and barely moistened his lips. Then he spoke only two words: "*Quercus robur.*" Latin for "oak." The wine we thought would rewrite Italian enological history and knock the French off their pedestal tasted only of oak to him. Wood. A sawmill. Another example: Tignanello soon landed on the wine lists of the top hotels and restaurants in my city. But Giorgio Pinchiorri, our friend and admirer and the owner of the celebrated Florentine enoteca that bears his name, almost came to blows in those early years with a traditionalist customer who requested that our new wine, which Pinchiorri had promoted and supported, be removed from his table and replaced with a "real Chianti."

Over time, Tignanello proved that once you set a course for quality, you should keep moving forward. Sassicaia was improving from year to year, and Solaia was added in 1978. It became clear that we had given birth to a new generation, a movement that would change the image of Chianti. In 2000, when it was announced that Solaia would be ranked number one by *Wine Spectator*, meaning that the Super Tuscans were officially going down in history, I said, "We wanted to rival France. But it would have been a mistake merely to imitate Bordeaux. So we made wines with so-called 'international grapes,' but in a Tuscan style and character. That's the key to the future."

In the late 1970s, though, classification was still an issue, especially when people outside of Italy began to insist that we had to define these wines, which didn't resemble anything they had ever seen. "Innovative table wine?" "High-quality table wine?" American journalists were the first to use the term "Super Tuscans" for wines that, while lacking the official seal of the area, were strongly identified with a historic vineyard and were clearly of extremely high quality. It was a good name, and a very American one.

The pioneering and historic phase of renewed Tuscan wines ended with another monumental Italian wine: Ornellaia. This wine was idolized in Italy and abroad. A pure red from Bolgheri made from very high-quality Bordeaux grapes, Ornellaia was created just steps away from the Sassicaia vineyard and our Guado al Tasso estate. My brother, Lodovico, who had left the company decades earlier seeking independence and new experiences, was strongly behind it.

This French-speaking Super Tuscan was made for the first time in 1981. It developed through a different route, though it, too, is the fruit of our beloved soil, the ancient estate of the della Gherardesca family where my mother lived. Legendary Russian enologist

André Tchelistcheff shaped the personality of Ornellaia. And this wine, too, was the result of a voyage—the idea for it was born in the vineyards of California, where Lodovico traveled to explore that market for our company. When he left the family business, his first project was to begin growing wine grapes on American soil. But his leading expert protested, "Why? You have the El Dorado of wine in your own backyard!"

Revised and perfected over the years, the vineyards where the grapes for Ornellaia grow follow the same credo as my own: the pursuit of quality and perfection. (Exactly one year after Solaia was ranked the Wine of the Year by *Wine Spectator,* the 1998 vintage of Ornellaia took that honor.) In 1986 at the same estate, my brother created another splendid wine, the very elegant Masseto, a 100 percent Merlot wine that has earned a place in the collections of all true wine aficionados. I like the idea that all the leading wines from that special time were made by descendants of one of our earliest known ancestors, Rinuccio Antinori.

In the years that followed, many people wanted to get into this successful category. Many suddenly discovered grapes from other countries and wooden barrels. Small barrels in particular became trendy—too often wines that didn't belong there were forced into them. (Renzo Cotarella once said in an interview, "A barrique is like a miniskirt—not every woman looks good in one.")

This isn't a technique that one learns on the fly. Just ask Giacomo Tachis, who in his writings explains in detail for many pages the correct type of oak to use, when and at what point on the tree to harvest the wood to obtain the perfect material, how it should be cut, which direction to place the staves, and how they should be "toasted." Without the right ideas, a sense of the proper schedule, and patience and passion, you just end up with wine that tastes only of oak, as Paronetto complained. Wine and food critic Davide Paolini later termed such wines "carpenter wines." Never slavishly imitate something because it's trendy. All wines are living creatures with their own personalities, and each is born, grows old, and ages in its own way.

Today I often hear that there are few true authentic Super Tuscans. Besides Sassicaia, Solaia, Tignanello, and my brother Lodovico's Ornellaia, the wines made with passion and a clear and well thought-out plan form a short list indeed. I'd include Isole e Olena Cepparello, the red Barberino Val d'Elsa "table wine;" Fontalloro, the red from Fattoria di Fèlsina in Castelnuovo Berardenga; Fontodi Flaccianello, aged in Panzano in Chianti and beloved by American critics; Castello di Fonterutoli Siepi from the Siena area; di Napoli Vigna d'Alceo produced on the Santa Lucia estate (with Giacomo Tachis's usual magic touch); and, finally, Le Pergole Torte, a Sangiovese created at the same time as Tignanello with love and perseverance by Sergio Manetti on the Montevertine estate.

Then there are four or five Super Tuscans from outside of the Chianti Classico territory, such as Lucia Sanjust's Galatrona and Ferruccio Ferragamo's Il Borro, and a handful of others in Montalcino, Montepulciano, and Maremma. The Super Tuscans as a whole are still developing, though they have won some major victories. Due in part to Sassicaia, originally considered a Super Tuscan, in 1994 DOC certification was created for the Bolgheri area—one of the smallest such areas in Italy. In 1984 and then in 2002, the famous

regulations for DOC certification of Chianti Classico that had frus-
trated us so were completely rewritten. Now nonindigenous grapes
can be used. White grapes can be left out of the blend entirely. New
techniques for selection, maceration, and fermentation of grapes
were taken into consideration. In a most satisfying paradox, the
1975 Tignanello would now be considered a Chianti Classico. In
other words, the current official blend of grapes in Chianti Classico
closely follows our recipe. This wine made the law, and not the
other way around.

Meanwhile, Tignanello has celebrated its fortieth birthday.
We've continued to improve it by working on the selection and distribution of plants. I think of the tortured moments from the late
1960s, the vineyards as they were then, and then I look at how they
are today. We currently grow six thousand plants per hectare, twice
the number we had back then. Each one produces fewer bunches
of grapes and is tended individually. These are prime noble plants
that may be healthful for one hundred years. Basically, we've tried
to reeducate Sangiovese. This variety that we know so well is sometimes too "exuberant." There can be too many grapes on the vines,
which leaves the plants fatigued and waters down the quality.

We've tried planting the grapes in less fertile soil in order to
bring them into balance, aiming for health over the long term. For
years we've selected the best plants in order to propagate them selec-
tively (in the beginning we chose thirty-five, then five). We've tried
and are still trying to farm different areas of the same land with
slightly different techniques and processes so that we can compare
the results over time. In the 1970s, the excellent and history-making
vines on the Tignanello estate still felt the effects of being over-
worked in the 1960s. Those in the 1990s, though better selected and

managed, were still "adolescent" in many respects. Only those we've worked on for the last fifteen years are now starting to get close to what I wanted.

After infinite tests and evaluations, today I want a vine every eighty centimeters (thirty-one and one-half inches). I want to harvest one kilogram (a little less than two and one-quarter pounds) of perfect grapes from a single plant, which will give me seventy-five centiliters of wine, which is the amount in one bottle: an exercise in Renaissance geometry, in pursuit of the "perfect vineyard" designed and described by Leonardo da Vinci in his famous treatise on the cultivation of wine that today is part of the collection in Windsor Castle in England. Perhaps now you understand how serious I was when I wrote about the P for Precision.

The 2004 vintage was good; 2007 was excellent and is only improving as it ages. Tignanello is a model of a high-quality wine and reinvented every season, because we continue to improve the vines and the vineyard, because we try always to provide support for nature and the many small variations in climate and soil, and because the same plants change their personalities almost imperceptibly as they age. The way they react to our actions and to what nature does also changes.

In the 1970s and 1980s, the Tignanello estate was my company's main open-air laboratory. Marchesi Antinori was expanding its markets and its land with excellent wines and with more commercial projects, such as Galestro, while we were also beginning to look for new vineyards in Italy and around the world to expand our views and our Chianti-born art. At the same time, work continued here, where small and seemingly infinite innovations were made to achieve a perfect Chianti.

That said, don't imagine some antiseptic bioengineering laboratory with workers in white coats and stethoscopes or electronic sensors on top of the poles in the vineyard. Improvement always begins with the nature of the vines and the place. Take the land, for example. One of the great things about the Tignanello estate is the widespread presence of not just marl stone, but also alberese stone. This white stone exists all over the region, from the pebbles on the bottom of the Arno to the Prato hills. It's played an important role in Tuscan history. The ancient Romans made lime from it; in the Middle Ages it was used to pave the streets of Florence; the striped Prato Cathedral is made completely of alberese stone, as are Prato's Palazzo Pretorio and Castello dell'Imperatore.

Alberese stone is a marl stone with manganese crystals. Its white veins enliven the Tuscan landscape. It is an excellent friend to grapevines, as it keeps the soil clean and refracts sunlight.

At the Tignanello estate we found large swaths of pure alberese stone. We broke them up and sprinkled them uniformly under the rows. This created a clean "floor" where no grass grows. Soil, stone, and plants are in direct and continuous contact with each other. We don't need to use any weed killer. Most important, that white stone that was ground and used by the great painters of the Renaissance reflects sunlight, bathing all sides of each row of plants in it. It's an inexpensive solution, in addition to being highly symbolic. Above all, it's natural. The relationship between the ripening of grapes and refraction of the sun has been studied at length by university agriculture departments, and a plastic film was invented that could be placed over the plants to optimize their natural exposure. We do that with our stone.

I'd like to say a few more words about the 2010 vintage. It wasn't an easy year. It was rainy, with long periods of excessive heat. We were forced to follow our vines very closely, and we feared until the last minute that we might have another year without Tignanello. But, as sometimes happens in our line of work, when we went to harvest the dark grapes from those vines, when we'd selected them, destemmed them, and placed them in the vats, they yielded exceptional results. The wine that's now resting in our cellars in French wooden barrels from Allier and Tronçais could be the best Sangiovese that I remember.

Sometimes I visit the Tignanello cellars and run my eyes over the rows of barrels lined up in the cool air. The Antinori cellars are a good example of that mix of innovation and pride in our origins that I've tried to describe in this book; that ability to remember and respect all Tuscan winemakers and all the Antinoris who came before us, while always being ready when faced with the challenge of a new vineyard to start again from scratch.

Beneath the sixteenth-century villa where some members of the Medici family lived before we arrived, down a stone staircase that starts from the ground-floor entrance, the ancient foundation created in 1346 by the Buondelmonti family—the first to live here—sits and waits. The old cellar with its soaring cross vaults is home to long rows of light wooden barrels. They are filled with Solaia, which shares its origins and its vineyard with Tignanello. It still needs to rest for at least eighteen months, and then it will sit in bottles in modern cellars not far from here for another year.

Further down a sloping hallway there are the Tignanello barrels, stacked under the curved plaster vaults. This is the heart of Chianti country. Meters above our heads, the Guelphs and the Ghibellines once battled. But don't be fooled by the mystical aura of this quiet place, the faint aroma of wood and wine—this is actually the newest part of the entire estate. We rebuilt it completely in the late 1990s, and then again in 2003. And we're still working on it, because I want the best for this wine.

We'll know soon whether the wine that comes from this place, from the harvest at the close of the first decade of the new millennium, will be the best Tignanello ever tasted, a wine that will make enologists and wine enthusiasts sigh with pleasure. Today, however, it's difficult to guess what the wine that we bottle in five, ten, or twenty years, or in 2071, when our Super Tuscan celebrates its one hundredth birthday, will be like. My grandchildren are the only ones who will get to see where this vineyard goes. Now, as always, we wait.

5

CERVARO DELLA SALA

Umbria and Tuscany

*W*ith aromas of very complex exotic fruits, a full and welcoming taste, and a big personality, Cervaro della Sala is made from Chardonnay and Grechetto grapes on the Castello della Sala estate in Umbria. Chardonnay grapes are typical of Burgundy, though they are now grown all over the world. Grechetto is one of the classic white grapes of central Italy. And Cervaro is distinguished, among other things, by the fact that it is one of the few Italian whites that can age for a long time with style. We opened the first bottles in the late 1980s, almost a half century after my father acquired the estate.

In 1350, nobleman Angelo Monaldeschi della Vipera built a castle four hundred meters above sea level atop a clay-covered, tuff-stone hillock not far from the border between Umbria and Tuscany. He was a litigious sort, and his ancestors split up into four groups so as to fight among themselves more efficiently. There were the Monaldeschi del Cane, dell'Aquila, della Cervara, and his branch, the della Vipera clan, who took their name from the word for "snake" and were said to be of the poisonous variety. The della Cervara counts who gave the wine their name lived on the land for a long time. Then the della Vipera family members moved in and took over. Eventually, in the fifteenth century, a marriage broached an agreement between the two families, who created a family crest that combined a snake, or *vipera*, attached to a deer, or *cervo*, by an umbilical cord. They lived happily ever after, or at least stopped fighting each other. The castle is an ancient and magical place in an area long famous for growing fantastic grapes for white wine.

Seventy years ago, on a trip to Naples, my father happened to discover that half of Italy wanted to drink white wine. In 1924, my father spent a lot of time traveling for work with a larger-than-life character named Umberto Cornia. Cornia was a rather grumpy Milanese who ate a lot, drank a lot, and dabbled in music and literature. He started out in Rome, then expanded his territory to pretty much all of Italy. He was a very determined salesman who'd stop at nothing to sell our wines. When he was dealing with a customer who had the temerity to refuse to make a purchase, Cornia would bellow, "*Sol chi non lascia eredità di affetti poca gioia ha dell'urna.*" (Basically, "On your deathbed, you'll regret what a miserable person you were.") He dragged my father along on a sales trip to Naples.

At the time, red wine was pretty rare in Naples. Our reds were on the wine lists of a few international hotels—but that was it. Fish restaurants lined the coast in and around Naples, and neither the tourists nor the well-off natives who filled their tables had ever heard of Antinori. My father and Cornia visited a restaurant near the port, and the owner whipped out a bottle of Orvieto (the generic term at the time for any white wine from Umbria) and asked, "Do you have any of this?" My father patiently explained that his family had been famous for its excellent red wine for centuries. The Neapolitan restaurant owner was unmoved. "People want a nice cold white to drink with fish," he said, and he politely showed them the door.

At the next restaurant, their offering of Chianti wine was once again rejected. "I want this," the restaurant owner said, holding a *pulcianella* (the squat, potbellied bottle typically used for Umbrian wines) of the standard Orvieto by its neck. "Can you sell me some of this?"

"Of course we can," Cornia answered without missing a beat. Before my father could protest, Cornia promised, "You'll receive delivery shortly." He took out a pencil and a pad of paper and began jotting down the order.

Cornia kept that up for the entire day. By the time the sun went down and they'd finished with their rounds, he'd taken orders for several dozen cases of Umbrian wine.

My father was getting worried. "Where am I going to get the wine you're selling?" he asked.

Cornia just smiled at him. "That's not my job. I handle sales."

My father, the future head of the company, certainly didn't want to leave all those customers in the lurch. He rushed back to San Casciano and urged my grandfather Piero (a man not fond of risks or surprises) to track down enough white wine to fill those orders. Somehow, they managed to do just that. The next year, they took a close look at Umbria, whose wines were so sought after by the Neapolitan wine drinkers. Maybe these customers were also looking for a viable alternative to Capri Scala, which was served everywhere in Naples back then.

My father's accidental fact-finding mission in Naples led to a new focus on white wine in terms of both quantity and quality. We used Trebbiano and Grechetto grapes from the areas known for those varieties, especially the area around Castiglione in Teverina, on the border between Umbria and Lazio. Then, in 1940, my father decided to purchase twenty-five plots on the Sala estate. He wrote later of that time, "I realized that simply parking ourselves on a hospitable local farm during the harvest wouldn't be sufficient to strengthen our presence in the Orvieto region."

The land he bought was in terrible condition. It would take fifteen years to set it right. By the early 1960s, however, those cellars were a model of innovation. Still, the castle, complete with medieval armor and frescoes, would only fulfill its destiny as the producer of a great white wine a good time later. I was glad that my father lived long enough to see his work start to come to fruition. Today, the cellars there remain ahead of the curve. They employ avant-garde techniques, and temperatures are tightly controlled. Mechanical pumping has been eliminated from the process completely; gravity does the work in the overhauled cellars. We also produce oil and goat cheese on the estate. It's an increasingly important spot in the Antinori landscape, a symbol of a new and different era.

The blends and quality of Solaia and Tignanello were perfected slowly. They were our signature wines in the late 1970s and early 1980s. But I'm equally proud of two wines from the following decade—two wines that proved Marchesi Antinori still had much to offer and wasn't going to rest on its laurels now that it was comfortable financially. The first was a truly perfect Umbrian white that reflected Renzo Cotarella's creativity and passion. The second was a Tuscan red from Guado al Tasso in the Bolgheri area, battleground of the Super Tuscan revolution.

Just as Giacomo Tachis—who isn't Florentine, not even Tuscan nor Piedmontese, and who had little experience with wine when I first met him—led the Tignanello team and left his mark on that wine and other wines created at that time, Renzo Cotarella's fingerprints are all over the Antinori wines from the later years. Both in chronological age and metaphorically, Marchesi Antinori CEO Renzo Cotarella falls exactly halfway between the Tignanello generation and the Antinori sisters, my daughters. I count myself extraordinarily lucky to have found him.

Today, Cotarella is an international wine star, but when I first heard his name in Orvieto, he was still a student. He divided his time between Perugia, where he was finishing up a degree in agricultural sciences at the university, and his family's small winery, where he did a little of everything. The year was 1977, and I was president of the Orvieto wine consortium. I'd gotten involved as a way to strengthen our ties with the region. The job of director of the consortium opened up, and I came across Cotarella's résumé in the pile submitted by candidates.

We met in July. I'd already heard that he was a sharp young man, and when I met him I saw instantly that it was true. Not only did he strike me as an excellent winemaker, but he struck me as an excellent person. He had the passion I look for when hiring. I pushed for him to become director over some better-known names. Though he was young and had only worked for his own family, and didn't have a fancy title or a lot of experience, I knew he'd do a great job.

For two years, the consortium thrived, in no small part because of the lively exchange of ideas between the two of us. The consortium was small and had only two employees, but it played an important role in the Orvieto area, long known for its winemaking.

Maybe subconsciously from the very beginning I was thinking of Cotarella's experience in the consortium's office as training for him to come work at Palazzo Antinori. In the late 1970s, I became convinced that he should be working for us. By then, Cotarella had earned his degree, with a little help from Giacomo Tachis. Our longtime enologist was one of Cotarella's idols, and Cotarella contacted him for some advice on his thesis, just as Tachis had once contacted his own idol, Émile Peynaud. That seemed like a good omen to me.

So I did something borderline improper that I've never regretted: I "stole" Cotarella from the consortium. On a trip to Orvieto, I made him an offer no winemaker could have refused—I asked if he'd like to be in charge of rebuilding the Castello della Sala estate. The cellars and the land needed to be groomed and improved so that they would be equal to our Tuscany facilities. He responded enthusiastically. We agreed that in the meantime he'd keep the director's position in Orvieto, because there was no replacement lined up and because I thought it wouldn't look right for the director of the consortium where I was president suddenly to become a manager at my company.

In 1979, Cotarella visited our estate in Umbria and toured its ancient tuff-stone cellars, fields, and vineyards for the first time. He's walked between the rows uncountable times since then, no matter what other commitments and responsibilities he has. For a few years, he divided his time between the office in Castello della Sala and the spot where I hoped to construct a model winery. We were constantly passing plans and proposals back and forth, whether on the phone, on paper, or in person. Some of those ideas needed to be fleshed out, and others needed to be streamlined and made feasible (a businessman's role in dealing with his most inventive and creative colleague), but most of them were intriguing. Cotarella's degree was in agricultural sciences, but he'd caught the enology bug. He fell in love with our company. "Both my head and my heart have always been intensely drawn to Antinori," he once said in an interview. My father, who was still alive at the time, met Cotarella and approved of my choice.

Cotarella has been with us ever since. Naturally, like all of us, he earned experience in the field before taking the helm of the company in 2005, and his responsibilities increased along with his experience. He started as consultant and director of Castello della Sala, and in 1998 he became general manager, responsible for overseeing all our production. In 2005 he was appointed CEO. He says that his various titles don't mean nearly as much as the fact that he gradually earned my trust and my daughters' trust. Indeed, my daughters see him as a big brother.

Cotarella's first assignment back then was to create a wine cellar, a vineyard, and eventually an avant-garde wine at that castle in Umbria. He was expected to achieve all that without damaging the castle nestled in the woods and its thirty-meter-high stone tower built in 1350. Initially, we aimed for "varietal redevelopment": going back to making the traditional local wines in an area whose climate and soil were among the most suitable in Italy for high-quality whites. The ultimate goal was to offer a product with a bigger personality and the Antinori touch. We conceived of it as "perfecting continuity." However, Cotarella and I would soon realize that we could set—and achieve—some more ambitious goals for ourselves.

Yet again, a dinner changed our outlook. I, my new enologist, and my friend Darrell Corti, a wine seller from Sacramento with an encyclopedic knowledge of the subject, were having dinner in the great French wine region of Burgundy. One evening, in a restaurant whose name I no longer recall, after a day in vineyards and cellars seeking inspiration for our white wines, we decided to order a wine that would offer a fitting ending to our trip: a Corton-Charlemagne, a Chardonnay with elegant aromas, aged about ten years. It was from Côte-de-Beaune, an area with low hills and calcareous soil.

That wine turned out to be exactly what we'd been discussing— a perfect white that could be aged for years. Not wanting the other diners to hear me, I leaned in close to my dining companions and whispered, "We'll never make anything this perfect on our land." Yet we did. As Cotarella has teasingly reminded me many times since, that evening the Marchese Antinori, who had defended Tignanello against traditionalist critics and fought so hard to regain control of his company, was ready to throw in the towel.

Fortunately, Cotarella was there to convince me that nothing was impossible if we worked with focus and perseverance. He argued that the Umbrian grapes were perfect, and the new cellars were ready to go. Years later, Cotarella told this story from a different angle. This is how he described the way "his" wine came about, in his own words: "A visit to Burgundy in 1981 led us to try something new. We discovered white wines that not only could be aged, but actually had to be aged to reach their full potential. A new dimension in the world of wine opened up to us, and we wanted to explore it." Optimism is another quality I would include on the list of requirements for the modern vintner. The upshot of the story is that when we returned home from France, we were no longer simply trying to add a few traditional white wines to the Antinori catalogue. Instead, according to Cotarella, we were looking for "a great wine that would offer character, personality, longevity. A wine with a soul that would represent the land and the producer."

To say that going from those ideas to actual wine in a bottle was complex would be a great understatement. However, we were free of commercial pressure, and we were no longer under the yoke of needing to turn a quick profit. Our young enologist could take as much time as he needed. We were going to try aging in barrels, a technique that we'd managed to get accepted in Italy for red wines. Aging white wine in barrels was unheard of and risky. There were no precedents. That was true of most of our techniques, such as cold soaking the grapes before fermentation (one of the secrets behind Cervaro's quality). Both Cotarella and I were disappointed in the first batch we made in 1982. He never gave up, though. He waited three long years for the right harvest (later he confessed that he despaired many times that he would never succeed), and in 1986 he tried again.

This time he focused more on Grechetto than on Burgundy grapes. To resolve the maceration issue, the grapes were harvested very early in the morning so that they would be cool (today we use a special machine for cold maceration that workers have nicknamed "the devil machine" because it emits big puffs of steam). He used only new barrels. He controlled fermentation more tightly. In short, he perfected the recipe. More than a century after my ancestors' initial attempt, we had our first high-quality white wine.

My daughter Albiera got her early training in those same cellars. This year her son, Vittorio, will be involved in his first harvest. And so it goes. This cellar is currently one of the most advanced, not just of the Antinori cellars, but in all of Italy. It relies on the philosophy of combining the modern and the traditional—the same philosophy we've applied to all our production. It's located partly underground and has a sloped roof that fits in perfectly with the hills. The cellars where Cervaro is made share the quiet beauty of the surrounding landscape. They are part of a quiet revolution—a perfect symbol of the man who has worked there since they were built.

Another unforgettable enological evening rounds out this part of my story. In London in the late 1990s, I attended a work dinner with producers from all over the world as part of the IWSC (International Wine & Spirit Competition). Each of us had to speak briefly about his wine, followed by a tasting. I was seated next to one of the great producers of Burgundy, who shall remain nameless, because, as Dante wrote, "'tis becoming to keep silent." He'd brought a white Montrachet from his award-winning French vineyard; I had my 1987 Cervaro della Sala.

When it was the French winemaker's turn, he began singing the praises of the wine in his glass: its color and light, its complexity, aroma, taste, and finish. Finally, my turn came. I tasted the wine in my own glass and discovered something odd: it was a Montrachet. I was positive. So which wine had the guy seated next to me been drinking? I realized they'd been switched. Everyone at the table had a good laugh. I'd been afraid I couldn't compete with the famous Burgundy wines, and instead my Cervaro was right in line with them. The French producer himself had said as much! More official confirmation: since 1988, all our Cervaro vintages except for 1991 (twenty of twenty-one vintages) have earned the highest rating of "three glasses" from *Il Gambero Rosso*, Italy's most influential food and wine magazine.

Tachis led Antinori through the era of the Super Tuscans; Cotarella has polished and strengthened the company, and he's not done yet. With Cotarella at the helm, Antinori has grown increasingly prestigious and garnered visibility—no small thing. Once I regained complete control of the company, I wanted to set new goals. Cotarella and I agreed that with a world of possibilities spread before us, we should never lose sight of quality. We could have made "easy" wines that would have been commercially successful; we decided instead to invest for the medium- and long-term in perfecting the formula for Tignanello. That called for extensive research on grapes, careful selection of raw materials, thoughtful experimentation, and reclaiming the essence of tradition.

We approached this in two ways. First, we expanded our search for the ideal terroir to the entire world, and second, we adapted our new winemaking philosophy to wine "habitats" in our home base. We started with Chianti Classico and then worked outward from there to cover Tuscany and eventually all of Italy. As Cotarella put it, the 1980s had been our commercial years, while in the 1990s our focus would return to production, albeit on a different scale and with different intentions.

I've already mentioned several times that balancing production and sales is key. We always aim to place equal emphasis on making the wine and informing the public about that wine. I'm no less than thrilled with what's happened over the last twenty years, starting with Cervaro della Sala. And though I've always considered myself a farmer at heart who loves nothing more than walking between the rows of grapes in a vineyard, I'm aware of numbers, too, perhaps due to my degree in economics (which my father insisted I study). My Antinori DNA kicks in when I'm working in the fields toward a concrete result and seeking to achieve my perfectionist ideals, and that background makes me somewhat unique among businesspeople. That's what Cotarella was talking about when he once told me that the Antinori world had seemed completely unique and even in some ways mysterious to him from the outside. "You're from another planet," he loves to tell me. In the end, I think the important thing is always to be yourself.

It always seems to me that the two different styles of our two great Antinori enologists in the postwar period depict the history of my company and all that it has achieved over the last half century. In creating Tignanello, Tachis carved out his own personal niche and "cheated on" Chianti to develop vineyards on Sardinia and Sicily. He did all that with our blessing, obviously. Before he came to Antinori, ours was a small company focused almost entirely on its native Chianti region. Understandably, his fiery vintner's instinct needed a larger stage and more varied spaces and stimuli.

For his part, Cotarella worked and created under the auspices of Casa Antinori, but he also reacted to the fact that by the time he arrived, the company was international and already quite diversified. That opened up many possibilities for him. "I could make wine in Chile, Hungary, Apulia, and California, while remaining connected to a company that fits me and reflects my ideals," he said. Things change. He works in a very different business than his predecessor did. Wine is more of a career path than it once was, and our company is large. Based on hectares of cultivated land and the number of grapes grown, we're probably one of the largest producers in Europe, and we're definitely one of the largest family-owned companies.

Yet we're still in touch with the land and the fields. That's been our approach since I realized that great wines can be created only by tracking everything, from planting the vines to tasting the final product. That has to be done on your own land and in your own cellars. The history of our company has been in large part a history of expanding our land holdings. Basically, our mission boils down to identifying the best place to make wine and then grooming that land so that it performs optimally over the long term. That's true whether the land in question is on the other side of the ocean or a half-hour drive from Florence. Terroir is key. This French word has acquired a complex meaning in wine terms. Today, it covers everything that goes into the creation of a wine, beginning with the vines planted. Everything must be done so that each wine, as Giacomo Tachis once wrote, is "unrepeatable."

When you encounter a new place where you've decided to produce wine, when you are trying to understand it, you need to consider the physical condition of the land, its exposure, its slope, the chemical composition of the soil, its microorganisms, microclimate, and pollution levels. But the landscape itself and the way it has been developed and shaped by generations of farmers also matter. So do the history of the nearby town or village, the kinds of animals that live in the woods on the other side of the hill, the kind of wine that's served in the area, and what local families eat for Sunday lunch. Everything about a new vineyard wields impact: the team that will work there, the plants and animals that will live around it, the cellars, even the color of the building that houses the offices. In our world, encountering new terroir, learning about it, beginning to work it, and seeing how it develops and changes gradually in response is a tremendously gratifying experience.

That's why we're still expanding. We began expanding in the Middle Ages. We've grown from our original little plot of land in Chianti to the rest of Tuscany and then throughout Italy. Actually, we're expanding faster and faster, because expansion is a constant source of opportunity and inspiration. Our ancestors discovered the same thing when they opened "agencies" all over Europe to develop their business. I like to think of acquiring and improving a growing number of Tuscan vineyards through our work as a way of redeeming them, of recovering land that was badly damaged by the winemaking crisis of the 1960s, speculatory building practices, and other modern evils.

In June 2011, when Italy crossed that historic threshold and produced more wine than France, I told journalists who asked me for a comment that quantity is meaningless. What's important is not that Italy can claim a growing number of vineyards and wineries, but that—as opposed to the situation forty years ago—they are high-quality vineyards and wineries. When grape growing and winemaking are performed to certain standards, they improve the land. Growth in high-quality vineyards always leads to greater harmony and fiercer protection of farming areas, as they are the laboratory and showcase for our lifestyle. A decrease in vineyards indicates impoverishment of the entire area. Planting a new vine anywhere is a form of investment in the future of an entire society.

You could even say that the Antinoris have taken back the countryside that was taken from them in the thirteenth century, when the castle in Combiate and its lands were destroyed by Florentine soldiers.

Yes, there was a "Palazzo Antinori" even then—only this one was a castle that sat in a strategic position between the Florentine plain and the Mugello area, near Calenzano, northwest of Florence. This was the early thirteenth century; the very young Florentine Republic was poised to become one of the most important cities in Europe. It would come to be the Manhattan or the Shanghai of its day. Florence was pushing to gain total control over the region. Less than one century after the name Antinori first appeared in an official document, this family of country squires was making its fortune selling fabric. The fact that the Antinoris lived in that ninth-century castle, which had changed hands many times, indicates that they were fairly influential and powerful. The details are murky, but what we know for sure is that Florence asked my ancestors to obey and submit. They refused. Antinoris were already firm and resolute characters who would not be deterred from reaching their goals.

The city's authorities were concerned the family might be growing a little too powerful. They wanted the Antinoris' business, and their florins, under the city's control. So in 1202 those authorities enacted a forced "acquisition." They sent a small army. After a brief siege, my ancestors surrendered. The army destroyed the castle stone by stone and issued a "public ban," according to fourteenth-century historian Giovanni Villani, "that the castle in Combiate could never be rebuilt." The only option left to my ancestors, if they wanted to continue to exist as a family (and carry on the family business), was to move into the city and live within its walls. They were forced to become Florentines. There, these former lords of the manor focused more intently on commerce. Basically we're a family of lapsed farmers who have returned to the land, and today we have a foothold in every area where great Tuscan wines are made. How did all this come to pass?

Let's step back a bit. We know that before the siege and destruction of the castle, Rinuccino Antinoro da Combiate, the earliest verifiable member of my family, made wine to be consumed there. This wine was almost certainly made of Sangiovese grapes, and the grapevines were then almost certainly destroyed in 1202. The first Antinori enrolled in the vintners' guild sold grapes and wine from other places. The Le Rose estate south of Florence, where Niccolò Antinori had built a Medici-style villa on three plots of land in the fifteenth century, made wine for centuries. And it was good wine, at least according to Tuscan literary great Francesco Redi, who referenced it in his seventeenth-century poem "Bacchus in Tuscany." In that era, the family also already claimed eight nice plots of land in Cigliano di San Casciano (where the grapes for the first Antinori sparkling wines grew), and other vineyards in the Prato area, in Valdarno, and elsewhere.

My father was the first Antinori to begin amassing land and vineyards in an organized fashion with the clear intention of providing raw materials for the family's wine cellars rather than relying on brokers to acquire grapes. My father's marriage to my mother, Carlotta della Gherardesca, brought the land in Bolgheri, the Guado al Tasso estate, into our portfolio. Guado al Tasso is on the Tuscan coast, ninety-six kilometers southeast of Florence. It stretches from the sea up into the hills.

The town is so tiny that it doesn't even form a municipality—it's simply a hamlet within Castagneto Carducci; in any case, it's so important in enological terms that it has earned DOC certification all its own and a well-deserved place on the Mount Olympus of wine. The town developed around a fortified castle that dates back to just after the fall of the Roman Empire. It seems to be have been the home base for a group of Bulgarians allied with the Longobards—hence the name. Then, for several centuries, all that land belonged to the della Gherardesca family.

So history played its part, but so did nature, by shaping the area into an absolutely ideal place for vineyards. During the days when the introduction of the first Sassicaia shook the international wine world, Émile Peynaud was heard to remark many times that he was amazed that a swampy coastal area known for humidity, fetid air, and mosquitoes could give rise to such well-structured wines. It's all due to the crown of hills that protects the vineyards, enclosing them in a perfectly formed amphitheater, open to the wafting scent of the Tyrrhenian and sheltered by thick woods overrun by wild boar. Wheat, sunflowers, and olives have always grown there. And wine has always been made there. Giosuè Carducci wrote of Bolgheri, "Through the town's streets / from the wine that bubbles in vats / comes the pungent scent of wine / to fill souls with joy."

We've only been producing wines there that surprised the world with their quality for a few years, though. We have one thousand hectares, three hundred of them planted with grapes, on land that ranges from sandy to clay-calcareous. There's a farm that dates to 1637 and nearby there are bits and pieces of various castles and many ancient guard towers that were once used to keep watch for Saracen pirates. There's also a swamp and a nature preserve that's home to deer, boar, pheasants, and the badgers that gave the vineyard its name, since *tasso* means "badger." As we've seen, Allegra's racehorses run in the Macchia del Bruciato nature preserve, along with the Cinta Senese breed of pigs that Allegra—who is truly the soul of our base in Maremma these days—raises in a semiwild state.

It's a unique place, and a place where my family has gone to relax for a half century. For generations, our vineyards have not just been places for producing raw materials, but our homes. And every time we have a chance, between our trips abroad and the travel that takes us from one end of Italy to the other, we head to our vineyards, far from the city and close to our grapes.

Tignanello served as our shelter during the difficult postwar years, and then it was "grandma and grandpa's house," where my children went to visit my father and mother. For one century, all the members of my family have gathered there each September for the harvest. The Umbrian della Sala castle is practically home to Renzo Cotarella, but also to Alessia, who lives in Rome, a quick one-hour drive away. Albiera got married in Badia a Passignano, an ancient estate and abbey acquired in the 1990s, in the ancient San Michele Church.

Still, Guado al Tasso has been our favorite country house for decades now. We've gone through several generations of horses and hunting dogs there. Each of my daughters has a house nearby today. We've gathered there almost every weekend for years. This was long before Bolgheri became a household name. Today, American and British visitors start swarming the area in late winter, looking for rooms in bed-and-breakfasts and tables in the local restaurants. Corporations from all over the world hold meetings there. All that was missing until the beginning of the last decade was a great Bolgheri wine from us, because before the Sassicaia revolution, we saw this as a place to make whites and rosé.

Renzo Cotarella and I worked long and hard on Guado al Tasso and its Cabernet Sauvignon, Merlot, and Syrah grapes. In 1990, it was ready. This red wine is as strong as the land where it was made, a Bolgheri Superiore that needs to breathe for several hours after it is uncorked in order to put its best foot forward. It is well worth the wait.

Today, Guado al Tasso is both our private refuge and one of the main laboratories where we explore our winemaking future. Indeed, many other wines were created there, including Vermentino di Bolgheri in 1996 (one of Alessia's favorite white wines—we have high hopes for it) and Scalabrone, a next-generation rosé that we named for a legendary rogue who is said to have lived in the area in the 1700s. In 1994, we built a nursery to grow precious rooted cuttings that can be planted anywhere. We have to keep a close watch on them, however, as the boars will eat all of them if given half a chance. The nursery also grows Vermentino, the excellent indigenous white grape from the Tyrrhenian coast, as well as new selections of Sangiovese, Cabernet Sauvignon, and Merlot that will be planted around the world. Our next great wine will probably stem from experiments we are conducting there.

Not far from Guado al Tasso, sulfurous water runs through the Maremma interior—one of Tuscany's most undeveloped and green areas. Two thousand years ago, it didn't look like this. This was the heart of Etruscan civilization. The area was dotted with thriving cities like Populonia. The Etruscans had a well-developed system of ports and roads, and they even had vineyards where they grew a precursor to the Sangiovese grape. Then the area lay abandoned for centuries. When the Lorenas reclaimed it, it came back to life. In 1995, we began to buy up land near Sovana, a city of clay and stone where the Etruscans sculpted tombs that looked like cathedrals into tuff stone (the Tomb of Hildebrand is perhaps the most famous). This is where Fattoria Aldobrandesca is located.

We grow grapes in this land of soft, volcanic tuff stone now. The Etruscans carved that porous stone to create temples, necropolises, and their extraordinary *vie cave,* or tunneled roads, as far as twenty meters below the surface of the rock. Such roads still crisscross the area, and people there still carve houses, restaurants, wine cellars, and garages out of the local stone. This area is also home to the Aleatico grape, an aromatic dark red variety that has existed for at least one thousand years. The vineyards on Fattoria Aldobrandesca stand to the southeast of the towers of the ancient city of Pitigliano, which perches atop a large spur of tuff stone and is known equally for its synagogue and a dry DOC white wine made with Tuscan Trebbiano. To the southeast looms Monte Amiata.

Our Etruscan vineyard has long yielded an Aleatico with the aroma of wild roses. After a bit of experience, we decided to try growing Malbec grapes there as well. French Malbec grapes—a Bordeaux classic—are soft and delicate, and they are rarely seen in Italy, though they've done very nicely in Argentina. The wine that resulted from this experiment earned a very respectable IGT certification (and still has room for improvement). We named it Le Vie Cave.

I like making wine in the land of the Etruscans. Tachis, a dedicated wine historian, told me that in Etruscan culture, daily life, spirituality, and waiting to go to the great beyond are inextricably linked. For the Etruscans, life was about preparing to move to another dimension. The afterworld was seen as a happy continuation of life. And wine was the thing that linked these planes, so it was absolutely central. Their houselike tombs were kept cool, as if they were wine cellars. Their funeral urns were shaped like amphorae. Vines and banquets decorate the walls in Tarquinia and are depicted on many vases in the Vulci Etruscan museum. (Vulci was an ancient city not far from Sovana.) Etruscan burial customs involved clothing and jewels, but also grape seeds. Basically, wine was involved in every Etruscan ritual and especially anything related to the gods. "Novices" were invited to drink a small amount of wine and get tipsy in order to enter into contact with the divine sphere of Fufluns (the Etruscan equivalent of the god Bacchus), and they all prepared to go to the great beyond in a joyful state. According to Roman writer Pliny the Elder, a statue of Jupiter made of grapevine trunks stood in the center of Populonia.

Etruscans had not vineyards, but vine "woods": they grew grapevines (it's generally believed that they grew *Vitis silvestris*) like small trees leaning against the trunks of larger elms. The wine Etruscans made would be considered undrinkable today. The grapes they grew were low quality, despite their sophisticated viticulture methods. Their wine was "hard" and dense, and they are believed to have mixed it with honey and aromatic herbs to make it drinkable and stabilize it. But I would still love to taste some.

The Etruscans brought the modern grapevine to continental Italy, probably from the East. They were also the first to export wine abroad. One hundred seventy amphorae of Vulci-style wine were found in a shipwreck off Cap d'Antibes. Yes, the Etruscans managed to conquer the market in Provence! Maybe that's why everyone in my family has always been fascinated by them. In the early 1900s, Gaetano Antinori was a major supporter and *lucumo*, or president (a *lucumo* was an ancient Etruscan king-priest), of the Etruscan Academy, founded in 1727.

The Tabula Cortonensis, a precious tablet that dates to the second century BC and was discovered in Cortona in 1992, contains the longest known text in the Etruscan language, and it references wine. In summer 2011, the Museum of the Etruscan Academy in the city of Cortona organized an exhibit with pieces from the Etruscan collection at the Louvre. The star of that show was "Arianna," an elegant bust of a woman in Etruscan-Greek style from the third century BC, which came from Paris. This statue of a woman from 2,300 years ago depicted its lovely subject, beloved by the gods, with vines and grape leaves woven through her hair. We commemorated the occasion (and the twentieth birthday of our estate in Braccesca) with an Etruscan menu of *moretum* (the garlicky cheese spread whose praises were sung by the poet Virgil), pasta with herbs, Tuscan boar in honey with farro polenta, leeks with sauce, and Etruscan cream.

We've continued to expand in Maremma. Our aims are twofold: to explore new terroir in an area that has proven so fertile for enology and to protect Tuscany and raise its profile further. Winemaking improves an area's environment; indeed, it can even save the environment. That idea is increasingly important to us. A clear example of this new and burgeoning commitment on our part is the Fattoria delle Mortelle, just south of the pine woods of Guado al Tasso. Since 1999, we've owned this natural oasis in the swamps of the Diaccia Botrona, inhabited by ducks, coots, and other migratory birds, not far from Castiglione della Pescaia.

Fattoria delle Mortelle sits on a hill about fifteen kilometers from the coast. The name comes from wild myrtle bushes, known as *mortelle,* that grow everywhere in the area. The Lorena clan that ruled over Tuscany until about a century and a half ago drained the swamps so that the land could be used for farming. My ancestors in Florence worked for a long time as officials and ambassadors for that noble northern family of enlightened men who made every effort to modernize the region. We are carrying on their work.

Grapevines were rare in the southern part of Tuscany before we got there. Eucalyptus trees—imported from Australia to central Italy a century ago to freshen the swampy air and shore up the soil—dominated the countryside. Blueberry bushes and large peach, plum, and apricot orchards filled the area, but it was basically virgin territory when it came to wine. In the hilliest part of the area, we created one of our first ecologically sustainable vineyards. It's quite high tech. The buildings are made of recycled materials, and we use low-impact glass and packaging materials.

We've transformed the land, removing most of the "foreign" trees and leaving the indigenous ones, which today are grown in compliance with organic standards. We knocked down abandoned industrial buildings and built a wine cellar in their place. Most of the wine cellar is underground so that it doesn't disturb the landscape. This is one of our new cellars, so it uses gravity to transport the wine from one place to another without mechanical pumps. An old farmhouse on the hill was left as it was after we restored it. Only then did we finally begin making wine here. We're still studying and improving these very young vineyards. For a few years we've made Botrosecco, a Maremma red, and white Vivia (the name of my granddaughter), which is intense and aromatic. My youngest, Alessia, our emerging enologist, is in charge of the farm.

So that's where our Tuscan vineyards are today. Along the sea between Bolgheri and Grosseto, the past and future of our presence in the Maremma are in Guado al Tasso and Le Mortelle. Just northeast of the Fattoria Aldobrandesca, on the other side of the border with Umbria, are the towers of Castello della Sala. Just south and east of Tignanello are Pèppoli and Badia a Passignano, which we took over in 1985 and 1987, respectively.

Then in 1990 we began working to acquire and relaunch the Braccesca estate. That land is located in Nobile di Montepulciano territory, between the cities of Cortona and Montepulciano. First it was Etruscan land, and then it was in the hands of the Romans. Later, it was the cradle of architecture and poetry during the Renaissance, due to the work of architects like Antonio da Sangallo, painters like Luca Signorelli, and poets like Angelo Poliziano. Above all, though, this is known as the native land of another mythical wine: Nobile di Montepulciano, made from Prugnolo Gentile and Canaiolo Nero grapes. The former is a relative of Sangiovese (some claim it's a variation of it), and the second is an ancient Tuscan variety. Both Voltaire and Alexandre Dumas wrote about Nobile di Montepulciano, which earned DOC certification in 1966 and DOCG certification in 1981.

We planted new vineyards and built a beautiful new cellar for our Nobile di Montepulciano, but the face it presents to the world, its label, still harks back to the past. It bears the old crest of the Bracci family that used to own the land: an armor-clad arm holding a sword.

In 1995, we acquired one hundred eighty-six hectares of woods and vineyards at Pian delle Vigne. Sixty of those hectares were planted with Sangiovese grapes. This estate is in the DOCG Montalcino area and in view of the Val d'Orcia. In 2000, we created our first Brunello there. We named it for the small local train station built in the 1800s and still in use today. Brunello di Montalcino was the most famous and widely available type of Tuscan wine in the 1990s. This intense red is clear and pure and uses only native grapes. The Brunello from Pian delle Vigne is yet another wine based on Sangiovese, my family's signature grape and our heart. Sangiovese is a deeply Tuscan grape and it's the one that we Antinoris have studied most closely, worked with most intimately, and most often paired with international grapes.

The Montalcino variety is an extremely powerful Sangiovese. The Biondi-Santi family selected it in the 1800s. They started with a clone called *Sangiovese grosso,* known as Brunello (literally, small and dark) because of its deep, rich color. The Biondi-Santi family has a long history in winemaking. They were vintners and humanists in Pienza. They've owned land in those hills for more than two centuries. They, too, battled vine disease. They, too, protected their most valuable bottles from the retreating Germans in June 1944. The Biondi-Santi clan hid its wine in a small room behind a false wall constructed quickly under cover of night by a loyal employee.

In the mid-nineteenth century, they had the same problem we Antinoris had—the same problem shared by all the large farms in Italy in that period to one degree or another. The world was expanding rapidly. Ships were faster and faster, trains were running everywhere, and commerce had gone global. International communication was now possible. But wine didn't fare well when it was stored in a hold, or exposed to fluctuating temperatures, or left to sit overnight in a customshouse. How many liters of Chianti turned into vinegar because of a one-week delay in a ship's schedule? Clemente Santi was the first to attempt to resolve this issue by working on the purity of his grapes. He invested much time and money. It was his grandson, painter and enologist Ferruccio Biondi-Santi, who at the end of the century first tested casks and refining techniques and in 1888 invented Brunello Riserva using the same formula that is still used today.

That wine paired and still pairs beautifully with good food. It has strong tannins that may even be off-putting at first sip, but then gradually grow on you. There are still two precious bottles of the first true Montalcino Brunello in the Biondi-Santi cellars at Fattoria del Greppo in Montalcino. They're the last two bottles in the world. They're one hundred twenty-three years old as of this writing, but according to the latest analysis, they are in perfect health.

In 1999, *Wine Spectator* included the 1955 Brunello Riserva Biondi-Santi on its list of the twelve best wines of the twentieth century. I'm pleased to note that the same magazine included our Brunello Pian delle Vigne in its Top 100 for 2002. In my opinion, Brunello di Montalcino, along with Chianti Classico, is one of the most balanced and long-lived manifestations of Sangiovese.

Speaking of the Biondi-Santi family, I would be remiss if I neglected to note that the family produced another great enologist, Tancredi, who was responsible for one of the best wines ever created in the Lazio region: Fiorano Rosso from the estate of Prince Alberico Boncompagni Ludovisi. This red wine was made of Merlot and Cabernet Sauvignon and aged in barrels. Veronelli wrote that "with the first taste, it burrows into your memory and makes you forever better."

This red wine brings us to another wine region, Lazio, and turns another page in my family's history. This part of the story began more than sixty years ago and has picked up again recently. It begins with a prince who passed away in 2005. He was the father of my wife, Francesca. Francesca and I got married in 1966 in Fiorano, near the ancient Appian Way. Our two families met through wine.

As we've seen, when the *mezzadria* system of farming was abolished, Italian agriculture would undergo a traumatic game-changing upheaval, especially in the central and southern regions. In 1950, the Italian government passed farm reform. Using funds provided by the United States under the Marshall Plan, the government began to redistribute some of the larger pieces of private property to farmers, often wresting land out of the hands of owners. This was intended to make the system more democratic and do away with ancient privileges and the class system—not a bad idea on the face of it. But as often happens when these things are dictated from on high, using timetables and methods that are invented by people who are not "in the field" but in an office somewhere, it didn't have the intended effect. In fact, it was decidedly negative. The forced reallocation of land was clumsy at best, and resources, traditions, and entire production areas were destroyed, never to be rebuilt.

Lazio and Tuscany were not left unscathed. A few of the long-lived vineyards in those two regions were able to save themselves, and they went on to be very important in Italian wine history. One was my father's. Another was that of horse and wine genius Mario Incisa. The Fiorano estate, of the Boncompagni Ludovisi family, was saved as well. It was no accident that these were the vineyards that survived. They'd been handpicked to serve as "model farms" that would be preserved to set an example for the rest of the sector.

In those years, the Boncompagni Ludovisi and Antinori families won a national prize for agriculture in the "large farm on the plains" category. The day of the award ceremony, my mother, Carlotta della Gherardesca, sat next to Alberico Boncompagni Ludovisi. The paths of our companies would cross again. The Boncompagni family was ancient and there were even a few popes in its family tree. Alberico in particular was a passionate producer who was always working to improve his wines. He was among the first in Italy to use French grapes and barriques, and he was also among the very first to adhere to the most rigorous organic growing standards. My daughters and I always picture him perched atop his enormous John Deere tractor—he insisted on driving it himself.

He was also a passionate horse breeder and was friendly with many of the famous jockeys of his day. He was one of a kind. Neil Empson, an American importer in the 1970s, once told me that it was useless to place a detailed order with him. "In the end, Alberico sent you whatever he wanted!" he recalled. At a certain point in the late 1990s, when my father-in-law was almost ninety and was not well, he realized that he couldn't personally oversee all the vines in the fields, but he also couldn't stand the idea of someone else taking over. So he made a drastic and impulsive decision that he kept secret from the many fans of his wine: he ordered that his vineyard be dug up.

When Luigi Veronelli heard about this tragedy in 2000, he was very upset, and he began trying to save the thousands of bottles that still sat in the Fiorano cellars, many of which had never been catalogued, as well as a small part of the vineyard. Those bottles ended up in the collections of major wine lovers and experts around the world as testimony to something that had vanished.

But wine always deserves a second chance. When my wife's father died, my wife inherited his entire property. With great generosity and wisdom, she decided to give part of the land where Fiorano was produced to our three daughters. She had only one stipulation: wine had to be made there again. My family took responsibility for bringing Fiorano back to life. It's the latest in our series of Italian wine ventures. Albiera, Allegra, and Alessia have just planted four hectares of vineyards near the original estate with the goal of producing a new Fiorano by 2015. Out of respect for their grandfather's philosophy, the entire vineyard is biodynamic, which means it uses some traditional techniques and adheres to standards that are in many ways even more rigorous than organic standards. Making wine that way is a challenge, to be sure, but it's invigorating, too.

By the end of the last decade, we were active in every major classic winemaking zone in our region. But we're not done yet. We're still gradually adding to our portfolio of Tuscan vineyards. And we've continued to grow. After the revolution in production and after years of commercial expansion, it was time to turn to producing a large number of new wines—and this time, we were going to do it far from home.

6

ANTICA NAPA VALLEY

Making Wines in the World

A glass of Antica Napa Valley Cabernet Sauvignon offers aromas of plum, blackberry, and raspberries. This wine is made from selected Cabernet grapes planted five hundred to six hundred meters above sea level in Napa Valley, northern California's "little Chianti." It is the first wine made at a 100 percent Antinori winery so far from Italy. It is also currently one of our main projects—and one of our most enjoyable.

The excellent Antica Napa Valley, which finally was ready in 2007, is, in my eyes, the latest proof that we made the right move when we set out to explore the world outside of Tuscany. Antinoris began working as wine exporters in foreign countries six centuries ago, but we only began making wine outside of Italy in the 1990s. Better late than never. Our move beyond the borders is one of the most interesting things the company has done in recent years. Vineyards outside of Tuscany that use our know-how—whether we planted them on our own or they were born out of a partnership agreement or investment—are a great work in progress in step with this era of increasing globalization. I really can't say where it will all lead.

As I've already noted, I like to travel. Tuscan farmers are not especially open to other cultures or exotic adventures. They tend to cling to their own little plots of land, their vineyards, and their convictions. But I'm descended from Florentine merchants who were traveling around Europe and creating branches as early as the fourteenth and fifteenth centuries. I am my father's son, and he was a salesperson and then an international wine salesman who in his own memoirs enthusiastically recounted his adventures going from one end of the world to the other—including his hospitalization on the outskirts of Athens with malaria (they "tortured" him with the local retsina) and customs nightmares in Istanbul when it was still part of the Ottoman Empire. He visited a South America populated by Italian immigrants, and crossed the Atlantic to New York aboard ships, never failing to explore their storerooms to see what they were doing with the wine. Every experience was an opportunity for learning. Travel was my father's mission and his obsession. He wrote, "After a while, I would always start to dream again of leaving; upon hearing the faraway sound of a train whistle in the darkest hours of the night, I would immediately be overwhelmed by a desire to pack up and start traveling to sell the wine that was aging in the San Casciano cellars."

Descendants of our branch of the Antinori family still live in southern Italy. These are the Antinoris who became the dukes of Brindisi—not the city in Apulia, but Brindisi di Montagna, a village up in the mountains of Basilicata. My ancestors arrived there in 1458, led by Antonio Antinori, who was a member of the court of Ferdinand of Aragon, King of Naples.

I know that for centuries the Antinoris in the Campania region bought and sold land, and the Santi Apostoli Church in Naples still contains busts of noblemen Fabrizio and Flaminio Antinori. Those Antinoris never made wine, but one of them was a very famous personality and world traveler: Duke Giuseppe Antinori, who lived from 1773 to 1856. He was handsome and liked to have a good time, and he managed to spend a large part of the family fortune on women, gambling, and carousing. He went on to become a very famous spy. First he served King Joachim Murat of Naples, and then he was an informant for the Austrian court and even the Russian czars.

When it comes to pioneering spirit, however, Orazio Antinori was without peer. He was a true multifaceted hero of conscience, and he was our ancestor, even though he belonged to the branch of the Antinori family that would move to Perugia in the eighteenth century. Born in 1811, he wrote that "few things are as intoxicating as heading to an unknown land." He was an ornithologist, a painter, a taxidermist, a naturalist, and an expert hunter, though once he was facing down a lion in Africa when he realized that he'd brought along an air gun by mistake. He was also an officer in several armies, a Mazzini-supporting liberal, and a Mason. He was both a deputy and a sharpshooter in the service of the nineteenth-century Roman Republic, a democratic experiment. After that experiment failed in 1848 and 1849, he declared that his native country made him sick and decided to spend the rest of his life in Africa.

While my grandparents were starting to export their first bottles to South America, Orazio Antinori was tirelessly exploring the shores of the White Nile and the Blue Nile, looking for specimens to collect or sell to natural history museums. By the age of forty-two, he worked full time as an explorer for the Italian government. At fifty-six, he founded the Italian Geographic Society in Florence. At fifty-eight, he was the Roman ambassador who presided over the opening of the Suez Canal. And at sixty-five, he led an ambitious and ultimately disastrous Italian expedition that set out to follow a route from the high plains of Ethiopia and Somalia—Italian colonies at the time—to the Great Lakes of the equatorial region. He died six years later, never having completed that final mission. A hunting accident and the endless fighting over borders between colonial powers got in the way. He always said he'd rather face an uncertain future from a Bedouin tent than live any other way.

Our family tree also includes a branch in Argentina, though we've almost completely lost sight of them. But suffice it to say that a passion for travel and new vistas is an Antinori genetic trait. Still, only the Antinoris of the last three generations have been so determined to put this attitude into the service of wine in Tuscany and in Italy. We have tried to do our best as both "vineyard vintners" and "market vintners." Indeed, my father was the only producer of his time who vaunted a dual passion for enological innovation and exploring new markets.

My whole life has been divided between these two things. In the beginning, I worked mostly as an area manager, first in Lazio and Campania, then in northern Europe, and finally in the Americas. So I was an administrator behind a desk in Palazzo Antinori and a winemaker on our estates in Umbria and Tuscany.

My daughters, too, performed apprenticeships far from Florence. They paired their faces and their names with our bottles for export.

On those trips they learned what they needed to perform their work in the offices and in the cellars, using what they'd discovered about taste and market evolution to make our wines better and more competitive. You could even say that a high-quality winemaker needs to analyze and then conquer a market in order to evolve. That may be more important than tracking down and planting a new vineyard. Basically, aspiring winemakers need to taste the world. They need to send out feelers. The more remote and—in the wine sense—virginal the land, the more exciting and enriching it will be to conquer it.

As I've already said, Canada was the far-off land where I was first tested as I traversed it with the Polish importer who worked for the KGB. Canada was my personal Far West at other times, too. I'll never forget a surreal trip I took to Edmonton, Alberta, many decades ago. In the lobby of what was then the city's only decent hotel, I unexpectedly ran into an old friend from Prato, businessman Felice Guarducci.

Guarducci had moved to Alberta with his family in the 1950s and it had become home for him. He knew the area well, and he spontaneously suggested that the next day, Sunday, we go on a little car trip to explore the countryside. We set off the following day in his car, but the term "countryside" turned out to be a bit of an understatement. We drove through wide swathes of desolate land for hours without seeing another living soul or even a house.

The needle on the gas gauge started to dip very low, and my companion realized we were miles from the nearest gas station. What to do? This was long before cell phones and GPS systems. All we could do was continue on and hope we would luck out. We spotted the outline of a farm in the distance. We agreed that the best course of action would be to stop and ask for help. We parked the car, and just as we were about to open the doors, a squawking white wave washed up around us. It was a gaggle of geese. I'm not talking about a few dozen geese, either. There were hundreds of enormous geese, flapping their wings and making a racket. They appeared to have been left there on their own, and they were very territorial. We had no idea what an army of angry geese could do, but we opted not to find out. I don't recall how we managed to find gasoline or even how we got out of there. All I remember is that even the farm animals in Canada are larger and wilder than ours.

More recently, I was fortunate enough to experience Canada through the eyes of Vinicio Ortolani, an Italian American who was very important to our company and to Italian wine in general. Ortolani was from Spello in Umbria. He was a trade officer at the Italian Embassy in Ottawa. Our personal ambassador, a man from Trieste named Smoquina, asked him to work on ways to promote Italian wine in that area. In the mid-1980s, Ortolani came up with a brilliant idea: a wine lovers' association, the Amici dell'Enotria, that would hold events and launch promotional campaigns to teach people about the culture of Italian wine.

The Amici dell'Enotria (Enotria is an ancient name for Italy and literally means "land of wine") formed chapters in the major cities. In just a few years, due to the passion and dedication of its founder and coordinator, it became a formidable advertising machine. Ortolani traveled and worked incessantly, and he was always coming up with new projects and new ideas. He was so busy that eventually he had to decide whether to work for the embassy or work for the association. He chose the latter.

I recall a couple of long trips crisscrossing Canada with him. These were an endless stream of meetings and evenings spent with numerous association members. All of them were attentive and passionate about wine, whether they lived in big cities or tiny towns. I met some colorful and extraordinary people. Ortolani was also behind that fateful tour of Italian producers that I described previously—my daughter Albiera's first time traveling with me and her "baptism by fire" as a representative of the company.

The only thing I didn't enjoy were the visits with honorary Italian consuls and other notable figures from our community abroad, and not because they weren't welcoming. Just the opposite. The Canadian state monopoly on alcohol was (and I believe still is) very strict about imports and charged high duties, but citizens were allowed to produce small quantities of alcohol at home freely for personal use without paying taxes.

I discovered that many Italian families took advantage of that opportunity. Most used grapes purchased from California and then made wine at home in honor of their native land. Of course, when I—not only Italian, but a winemaker—showed up, the first thing they did was pull out their wine and ask me to taste it. They wanted to know what I thought of it and they wanted some encouragement in their endeavors. In all my travels throughout Canada, I never once tasted a homemade wine that was even close to decent. Obviously, out of respect for my friend Ortolani and our hosts, I could never say a bad word. Frankly, the stuff they made was swill, but I would act out a professional tasting, then find something positive to say.

My daughter Alessia feels that the time she spent in New York helped her develop important contacts, but her years based in Hong

Kong and working throughout Asia, the Middle East, and Oceania were her true formative years. She was there about ten years ago, at a time when few Italian producers braved those shores, and those that did limited themselves to Tokyo, Beijing, and Singapore.

Alessia once counted the flights she'd taken in a month and found she'd been on a plane a whopping twenty-three times. She went to Thailand, Cambodia, Korea, Vietnam, the Philippines, Malaysia, and southern China. Not only had no one in those places ever heard of Antinori, but they didn't know where Tuscany was or how a table wine was meant to be used. The few bottles on the tables of very fancy international restaurants and hotels contained Chardonnay from Australia, which was relatively close, or the usual Bordeaux wines.

Alessia would call and report back to me about meetings with the importers who in theory were responsible for selling our wines. Sometimes while talking to them, she'd realize they had no idea that there were red wines and white wines, or that some wines should be refrigerated while others were to be stored at room temperature. But she also told me how exciting it was to start from zero with people and explain the entire world of wine to them—what a vineyard is, or a barrel, and how quality is determined. She was a young female blank slate to them, as the Antinori name meant nothing.

"It forces you to figure out the essence of what you do and who you are," she told me. And seeing people take even baby steps was encouraging. She met Cambodians who had lived in the West while a long series of wars and dictatorships roiled their native country. In the mid-1990s, they returned home in the hope of modernizing Cambodia and teaching their peers about, among other things, wine. The Chinese evinced a genuine interest in high-quality food and wine, and they were starting to become aware of Italy as a style leader in many fields.

Selling wine and making wine in unexplored territory bring similar challenges. Cultivating a vineyard in a foreign country automatically educates people there about your brand. You can break the ice by working with local winemakers and selling wines made from native grapes that reflect the local spirit. Many of our new wines made outside of Italy are available solely in foreign markets, with an eye to globalization. Entering new territory helps you expand your audience, plus you assemble a long list of future terroir possibilities. You just have to go in with open eyes and an open mind.

This bears repeating: the vineyards outside of Italy that we own or are partners in still account for a small portion of our total production, and our sales in these emerging markets represent a small portion of our revenues. Tuscany's Chianti Classico area is our production, cultural, and emotional center, with a few locales across the border in Umbria and the Maremma area. Our major markets are still Italy, North America, and Europe. But it's important to maintain a presence in Hong Kong, Phnom Penh, and Canberra. It's important to test the waters, to lay the foundation. You always need to be looking for new areas. I wrote earlier in this book that passion is at the top of the list of qualities that a true vintner possesses, but Renzo Cotarella would place a different item in that top spot: curiosity.

The name of the Antica estate in Napa stands for ANTInori CAlifornia. We fell in love with the land at first sight, but that initial impact was followed by a long, slow courtship and an exchange of vows that only yielded its first fairly scanty results a few years ago. The secret was patience. I first laid eyes on this plateau of land that seemed designed for winemaking in 1985. Whitbread had asked me to cross the Atlantic to serve as wine expert.

There were five or six local vineyards for sale. They seemed suitable for producing the kind of wine that appealed to the British, who wanted to bolster their presence in the United States. When they called me from London in August, I was on vacation, but I made the trip anyway. Something new and exciting was happening in the hills north of San Francisco, and I'd been meaning to check it out for a while.

California had burst onto the international wine scene in 1976, at what is known as the Judgment of Paris. There, at a blind tasting (meaning the judges didn't know the names or the provenance of the wine they were tasting) with leading French experts and sommeliers, a group of California Chardonnays and Cabernet Sauvignons—most notably those from Chateau Montelena and Stag's Leap Wine Cellars—had outclassed similar wines from France, to the shock and horror of the French.

After all, the French created enology, the terminology still used today, and the mystique that surrounds it. As my father once wrote, the French were masterful at "glorifying their own Bordeaux châteaux and Burgundy crus. In Dijon, they speak of a certain Colonel Bisson, commander of a glorious infantry regiment, who during a march toward a war zone passed before a splendid Côte d'Or vineyard. He stopped his regiment and ordered them to present arms while the brass band solemnly beat its drums." Wine was a symbol of French national pride, and the Judgment of Paris was a shocking turnaround. All of us who were making wine in the Old World began to second-guess ourselves and our presumed superiority.

For me personally, the quick progress in Californian wine-making was no surprise. I first visited Napa Valley in 1966, and Giacomo Tachis and I had been making the rounds of the more highly regarded California estates since the early 1970s, when we were working on Tignanello. We'd been won over immediately by the pioneering spirit of California winemakers—a breath of fresh air for us as we dealt with intractable fellow winemakers and wine buyers back home.

One of our first guides in this new area was Darrell Corti, a dear friend I've already mentioned. This well-known wine seller from Sacramento, whom we'd met for the first time in Italy, was a kind of walking encyclopedia of food and wine, and not just California wine either. Corti was the kind of Italian American (his grandfather emigrated from Genoa) who is completely American, but remains fiercely proud of his roots. At that time in the United States there was a growing group of third-generation Italian Americans who were researching their family histories and renewing ties to Italy.

The grandparents of that generation had experienced misery and exclusion, and in response they'd worked hard to erase any trace of Italian culture from the children they bore on American soil. They wanted their children and grandchildren to fit in, so they encouraged them to play with American kids, and they jettisoned Italian traditions and made great sacrifices in order to send their offspring to study at the best universities. In the 1960s, it was common to meet young Americans with Italian last names who couldn't speak a word of Italian. Darrell Corti and others like him were attempting to reverse that trend. As an adult, he learned to speak not only fluent Italian, but perfect Genoa dialect that sounded as if he'd been raised on that city's winding streets.

Corti accompanied us on most of our American exploration. He knew all the producers in California personally and was invited to all the conventions and tastings. He was an excellent wine critic and had an incredible palate. Once when Corti was my guest in Italy, he did something that blew me away. Mario Incisa, the creator of Sassicaia and my uncle, friend, and inspiration, continued to produce his own personal version of Sassicaia after Tachis became the winery's enologist and made the wine widely available in commercial form. On the sly, Incisa secreted a small portion of the grapes in a private area in the cellars, and there he made his own wine from them, just as he had for years before the boom. Each year he produced no more than a couple of barrels of his Sassicaia, then transferred it to bottles (he even drew the labels by hand) that were later doled out to a few close friends, including myself. He called it "different Sassicaia wine."

One evening when Corti was visiting, Incisa poured him a glass of that "anarchist" wine, which had never been available for sale. He didn't say a word. Corti immediately identified it as Tuscan. Then he narrowed that down to Maremma. He thought perhaps it was a Sassicaia, but then he tasted it again and noted that there was something strange about it, something unexpected. Finally, he asked, "Is this that 'different Sassicaia wine' that the Marchese Incisa makes each year on his own?" He'd nailed it. We were amazed. I hadn't even realized that anyone outside of our small circle knew about my uncle's quirky winemaking adventures.

At the dinner for Tachis at Palazzo Antinori, Corti told a story about the first trip we three made in California. We stopped to grab a sandwich in a place that didn't serve wine. Corti was afraid his Italian visitors would be offended by the idea of a wine-free lunch, so he took a bottle out of the trunk of his car for us to share. Naturally, he had a little surprise in store for us: a red wine made in Napa Valley with Barbera grapes. He opened it and we drank, and then he handed us the bottle. Apparently, Corti was highly satisfied to see that Giacomo Tachis, talented creator of so many of the great Piedmont reds, was impressed. Raising his eyebrows, Tachis said, "I knew they made great Cabernet here, but I had no idea they made Barbera that's better than what they make back home." I don't recall the label on that bottle, but I'll never forget the aroma and quality of that American Barbera.

Our strong relationship with the United States and Americans may seem incongruous at first glance—what do the descendants of a twelfth-century family of merchants from the Florentine country-side have in common with the inhabitants of a country formed out of revolution only a couple of centuries ago? My daughter Allegra believes that our family's "American blood" plays a part.

My mother, Carlotta della Gherardesca, was three-quarters American. Her mother and her grandmother were both American. My mother loved Italy and Tuscany, but her sense of civic duty and the generosity that she worked to instill in us were purely American. She was an extraordinary person. Though she knew nothing about wine, she taught us that when you are born lucky—either due to your family, your personal success, or plain old good fortune— you should never forget those who are less privileged. Good luck should be repaid. She was a great patron of the arts and a dedicated philanthropist. When she inherited a villa near Florence from her mother, she turned it into a children's hospital, Istituto Principessa di Piemonte. Before health care was nationalized in Italy, children of lesser means were treated for tuberculosis and other diseases there. Today, it provides hospice care for the terminally ill. Our family still supports it heavily, and it still bears our name.

My paternal grandmother, Natalia "Nathalie" Fabbri, also had American roots. She was descended from a Florentine family that made its fortune in America. The enterprising Fabbris arrived in New York in 1851. They began selling silk, but then became ship owners, financiers (they partnered with J. P. Morgan), and patrons of the arts. Egisto Paolo Fabbri, an American Tuscan who was born and died in Florence, was one of the founders of the Metropolitan Opera in New York. The Fabbris are the link that connects the Antinoris to the Italian immigrants who helped build the foundation for the modern United States.

Natalia met my grandfather Piero after part of the family returned to Florence. She married him and lived the rest of her life as an Italian citizen in the Tuscan capital. When she passed away, she left lovely watercolors of the historic center of Florence. My grandfather Piero saw the early skyscrapers rising in New York and hunted moose in the Canadian forests of New Brunswick back in 1906. Then my father traveled throughout North America as well, in his persistent attempts to conquer the market. Finally, I grew familiar with California and New York.

Those two places are very different from one another, and we are privileged to have gotten to know both California's relaxed lifestyle and gently rolling hills, and Manhattan's pulsating nerve center. The former is where wine is made, but the latter is the place to go to acquire new contacts, talk about our work, hear the latest buzz, and get a handle on fashions and styles. This same dichotomy between the East Coast and the West Coast of the United States is echoed by the dichotomy in my own work (perhaps even in the work of every businessperson in this global era): on the one hand there is the productive/creative aspect of the work, and on the other the sales/business aspect.

In order to win over this gigantic market, you need to know about the latest bottles from winemakers in Napa Valley and Sonoma Valley. It's interesting to harvest with local producers; having your own vineyard under the California sun will certainly help you understand the area's wine more deeply. But that's worthless if you don't know how to talk wine in New York. You need to know about the most influential oenophiles of the moment, the most highly respected critic, the most stylish restaurant. You can find any kind of food or drink in New York. If something is happening in the world of food and wine—from a new wine to an experimental concept for hotels or restaurants—it happens there.

In New York you'll find the best of everything, because the city is a showcase viewed by the entire world. It's also an enormous open-air gym where people build their business muscles in an electric atmosphere of global competition. You must have a presence there. That's why my daughter Alessia lived in New York for several years. The permanent presence of an Antinori continued a tradition that began with my grandfather and father at a time when the United States market was still mysterious and remote and we had more luck selling in Latin America. In Alessia's first year working in the Big Apple, she added fifty or so new New York restaurants to our customer list. It was a clear sign that we'd made the right move.

All my daughters have worked in sales around the world. Again, approaching new markets, learning about trends, and using our name as a calling card are all key. The world is changing. It's getting faster and bigger, and the real and the virtual often stand side by side, but selling wine has relied on the same basic premise since my father and I made our first trips abroad: the ability to relate and manage human contact. It's all about the trust that you inspire with your face, your style, and your word.

Alessia is perhaps the one most immersed in this mission, having found her vocation across the Atlantic. Indeed, my youngest daughter encapsulates the duality that I've tried to explain. She's a born enologist who spent years working on Montenisa Franciacorta, but then she wanted to do something different, so she headed out to promote our wines in the larger world. Recently she had a baby, and since then she's spent most of her time at home in Rome. This may be the turn of events that pushes her to get back to the cellars. We'll have to wait and see.

All the Antinoris who have lived and worked in the United States recognize that everywhere in that country—whether in the vineyards or in the big cities—there is an air of optimism, a mix of creativity and business sense, enthusiasm and commitment, the electricity of a society in perpetual motion, where merit is rewarded over background or an impressive last name.

Americans tend to see challenges as learning opportunities. A few decades ago, the only Americans interested in wine were Italian immigrants. Today, people of varied backgrounds all over the country share widespread enthusiasm for wine. Americans eager to learn about vineyards and cellars tend to take a more methodical and humble approach than Italians do. To some degree, every Italian considers himself a wine expert (not to mention a soccer expert). But in the United States, wine isn't a given the way it is in Italy. Americans didn't live through the era of wine on tap, or everyday red or white table wine. They think of a bottle of wine as a precious object synonymous with refinement. I think the global market is headed in the direction of the American market: fewer drinkers, fewer bottles, but higher quality.

Some Italian regions have developed or are working to develop wine tourism—creating itineraries and museums—but wine tourism is an almost wholly American invention, born in places like Napa Valley. Even in the very early days of the American wine boom, families visited vineyards to learn what went into the bottles they bought to celebrate important occasions and then kept closely guarded in the coolest spots in their homes. Wine tourists all over the United States equipped themselves with guides, cameras, and notebooks. They made pilgrimages to the places where their country's best wines were made, just as they would have traveled to see an art museum or a religious shrine. They were all like Colonel Bisson on leave, spending money and traveling for miles to look, ask questions, and touch with their own hands. The concept of a winery as a place that interfaces with people and with the world is an American one.

On the flip side, the American admiration for all things Italian is sincere and touching. Americans have such a desire to understand and learn our style that when they visit Italy, they leave full of ideas and energy. For an Italian businessperson, to see Americans in action this way is to be reminded of the values that made Italian craftsmanship great: creativity, an innovative spirit that still honors tradition, the ability to make something out of nothing, and the opportunity to work within a unique and organic cultural system. Thanks in part to Italian immigrants to American shores, Americans still see Italy as a place to experience *la dolce vita*. The citizens of that world superpower adore the mosaic that is our nation of thousands of local souls and thousands of different cultures.

If I had to name the one thing that I envy most about Americans, it's that they are blessed with a bureaucratic system that is a help to producers rather than a hindrance. Their system doesn't trip them up with an overload of rules issued by an army of different offices and bodies. In Italy, the rules are rarely clear. Indeed, they're often confusing, and frequently they contradict each other completely. In the United States, the few laws about wine that do exist are clear, and everybody follows them. My daughter Alessia says that there are still plenty of Americans who have yet to discover fine wine. There is still an untapped audience.

I've gotten a little off track here, but what I wanted to tell you is that when I was called to offer advice on an investment in Napa Valley, I already knew the United States, its people, and its wine. Through Darrell Corti, I'd met Robert Gerald Mondavi, the father of the American wine revolution and the first man to understand the full potential of Napa Valley after the fourteen dry years of Prohibition, when the Volstead Act absurdly banned the production, sale, importation, and transport of alcohol on American soil. Mondavi's parents had emigrated from the Marche region of Italy and got involved with wine by transporting grapes from California to the East Coast. Then they bought the local Charles Krug Winery. Mondavi had a brother, and at a certain point they split. He believed in family companies, but after a round of arguments, he was no longer associated with his parents' winery. He began to make wine on his own.

Mondavi's company, like mine, was designed to last for generations. He founded it in 1966, the same year that I took my position behind the main desk in Palazzo Antinori. Mondavi was already fifty-two at the time. He created Robert Mondavi Winery and generated numerous ideas for quality, marketing, and packaging at an age when many are looking forward to retirement. Mondavi loved wine with the passion of a perfectionist, and he never rested on his laurels. He's often remembered as the first American determined to produce high-quality wine, but he also had solid financial training, and he was an excellent communicator.

Like us, he dreamed of achieving excellence that would outlast any trend. He was free of the timidity that reverence for ancient European traditions can inspire. Indeed, he relished competing with that world of an almost infinite number of small companies as they competed against each other and suffered from provincial attitudes and blind loyalty to place. He created something out of nothing. Basically, he gave birth to the American high-quality wine industry and built it on a foundation of research and shared knowledge.

Mondavi was generous and contributed a great deal of time and money to raising the profile of Napa Valley. He was also instrumental in creating a department of viticulture and enology at the University of California, Davis, in order to leave something to the producers who would come after him. That was instrumental in making California a winemakers' paradise. He also financed the arts, restored theaters, and reinvented wine tourism with Copia, the American Center for Wine, Food, and the Arts in the city of Napa.

Above all, Mondavi gave us the gift of unforgettable wines of exalted quality that could compete worldwide.

This living monument to American enology was a very important figure for us. The example he set and his experience with winemaking influenced us greatly during the years when we were figuring out the early Super Tuscans. Mondavi had a different kind of impact than Émile Peynaud, but he was just as inspirational. In the 1990s, he warmly welcomed a seventeen-year-old Allegra to his winery so that she could earn her stripes in the field. Extremely open-minded and generous, he never hesitated to include her in his research and his experiments.

Robert Gerald Mondavi passed away in 2008; he was a charismatic and visionary man in the mold of the American pioneers of the previous century who hunted for gold and tamed the wilderness. Maybe that's why, according to my daughters, I always returned from my trips to California full of newfound optimism and ready to roll up my sleeves. Mondavi and I were good friends for a long time and always had great respect for each other. He even participated in Ornellaia. He followed the Super Tuscan revolution and loved Italy and its wines.

Anyone who's interested in wine must read Mondavi's autobiography, *Harvests of Joy*, in which he describes his life as the fulfillment of the American dream. His philosophy in a nutshell: in this country, in a climate where spirit and character are always valued, your life can change in an instant and you can do anything you set your mind to if you persevere and stick to your vision.

Unfortunately, there's also a less cheerful book about Mondavi, *The House of Mondavi: The Rise and Fall of an American Wine Dynasty* by Julia Flynn Siler, which recounts recent history. That book speaks of financial issues, image problems, and disagreement among the next generation at the largest winemaking company in the United States. Robert Mondavi had a daughter and two sons, who suffered irreconcilable differences. Also, the company was listed on the stock exchange, and perhaps it failed to reconcile consistent style and quality with the demands of stock analysts. The fact that my friend's incredible legacy—in both human and business terms—was lost in a matter of decades has weighed heavily on the minds of myself and my daughters as a cautionary tale.

None of the vineyards I visited in California in 1985 seemed like a sound investment. Just as I was about to return home empty-handed, I was asked to assess another vineyard. On my last day in the United States, I found myself on the twisting Soda Canyon Road in a slightly isolated area, with a semihidden and almost virgin valley spread before me. There were just a few rows of grapes planted; the rest of the land was uncultivated.

I don't know whether I really have what Giacomo Tachis has termed the "Antinori gene," a sixth sense for reading land and seeing its long-term potential. Renzo Cotarella, who has accompanied me on all my exploratory missions investigating new property since the 1990s, says you should never go see a new vineyard with the intention of buying it. You should just plan to get to know it.

Exploration of new land must be guided by the proper combination of intuition and preparation, passion, and, last but not least, curiosity. Often these encounters are guided by fate or sudden inspiration. It's almost as if the vineyards want to meet me. On that estate a few miles from the Pacific, I saw something. The arid landscape of rolling hills had all the signs of a strong vocation for growing grapevines. It very much resembled the Chianti countryside. The rocky soil on the slope formed a natural amphitheater; the altitude and the cool breeze off the ocean reminded me of home. The light, however, was different, the horizon broader and sharper. It was the light of the New World.

That first encounter was followed by years of work. At my suggestion, Whitbread purchased the land with a small investment on our part and on the part of Champagne Bollinger, and it lavished a lot of money on radically transforming it. As advisor—not to mention owner of 5 percent of the property—I followed the developments closely and with great excitement. By the time Whitbread decided to bow out of the wine business, the work was almost done. I held on to my 5 percent and waited patiently. When the new owner, a large financial group, offered to sell us the estate, it was like Christmas come early for me and my daughters. Negotiations among us, the owners, and the bank that had to agree to the transaction were long and drawn out, but in 1993 we acquired the estate, three hundred hectares of vineyards in all. But there was a hitch: we had to lease the land back to the old owners for another fifteen years, a system that would help them with their balance sheet (they were listed on the stock exchange and had to maintain a certain level of return on investment) and would help us pay the mortgage. Basically, I owned a California vineyard, but I couldn't do anything with it. I was chomping at the bit. Then there was another twist.

Bordering on the land that we couldn't use was another small piece of land, about ten hectares, with the same characteristics. It was perfect for starting to experiment with our American wine. We tracked down the owner, a certain Ms. Townsend, a ninety-year-old widow who raised hens there and lived on the land in a house where she had spent her entire married life, surrounded by eggs and chicken feed. We tactfully asked whether she would be willing to sell, assuring her that she could keep her house. She named her price, which was a fair one. We thought we were good to go. But then she added a caveat that threatened to scotch the whole deal: "Just promise me that wine grapes will never be planted here."

We were stunned. At first, we thought someone was playing a joke on us. But Ms. Townsend could not have been more serious. She was a member of a strict local evangelical church. Indeed, she was so devout that she planned to leave the church all her property and the money from the sale when she died. And she and her fellow church-members considered alcohol an affront to God. After talking things over with her pastor, she'd decided that allowing wine to be made on her land—remember, we're talking about land in Napa Valley—would be an unpardonable sin. "You can grow table grapes, or grapes for grape juice," she suggested as consolation. "Grapes really thrive here. Did you know that?" We knew that. She would not budge. A woman born at the turn of the century was shaping up to be a more formidable negotiating adversary than many large corporations.

Glenn Salva, my trusted advisor in Napa Valley since 1986 and today the manager of Antica, visited Ms. Townsend and spoke to her many times, but to no avail. Then he had a brainstorm. He told her, "Okay, we'll plant table grapes, but since table grapes only bring in one tenth what wine grapes bring in, we'll pay you one tenth your price." She thought about it. She hemmed and hawed and put us off. Perhaps she consulted her pastor yet again. Finally, she said, "Okay, you can plant wine grapes!" We were overjoyed. As soon as possible, we planted grapevines where the chicken coops had once stood.

The first Antica Napa Valley Cabernet Sauvignon was harvested in 2004. Ripe fruit from land that had delivered what it promised: a perfect valley, where today Chardonnay grapes can be grown in the lowest area and Cabernet and Sangiovese in the higher parts. Our family of city dwellers and travelers, explorers and ambassadors, whose members in the mid-1400s already sold silk in Bruges and Lyon and a century later did business in Flanders and Toledo, whose members had traveled everywhere from Argentina to Turkey, now had its California winery.

Meanwhile, when I served as judge in a wine competition in Seattle in the 1990s, it set off another American adventure. I was surprised to discover that the interior of a state best known for salmon fishing offered excellent grape-growing conditions and a proud—if nascent—winemaking tradition. Elegant wine with enough personality to compete with European vintages was being made in those hills with their mild climate. I felt at home there right away, and on later trips to the United States I always tried to include a stop-off in that part of the country so I could taste the work of local producers.

At the suggestion of our friend the great Russian enologist André Tchelistcheff, we contacted Chateau Ste. Michelle, a Washington winemaker in business since the mid-1960s. After lengthy discussion, we formed a partnership—the first in this part of the United States between a historic European brand and an American brand. Then we embarked on farming and winemaking experimentation that combined our methods and their grapes. We planned to start a small project together from scratch.

Since 1995, we've produced Col Solare, a red wine designed for the American market. This is the first wine in my career that was a true collaboration. My partners and I chose the best grapes from six different properties and built a new wine cellar dedicated to this wine. We all learned a great deal from the experience. Today the Col Solare estate is a small, high-quality company geared largely to the domestic market, but it has the potential to grow. Forming a partnership with a passionate local producer is the only way to understand and comprehend another winemaking environment. This work gets you out of a provincial and closed mind-set. Each terroir has its own issues, so each one offers a learning experience. Contact with a different "wine school" always helps broaden your horizons.

We recently formed another American partnership with Warren Winiarski's Stag's Leap Wine Cellars, one of the best in Napa Valley. Previously I wrote about the Judgment of Paris, the French-American wine contest that rocked the wine world. It was a wine made of grapes that grew and ripened and then were pressed, fermented, bottled, and aged here, a Stag's Leap Wine Cellars 1973 S.L.V. Cabernet Sauvignon—little known at the time—that on the fateful day of May 24, 1976, humbled French masters by earning the highest ranking: a stratospheric 127.5. Today a bottle of that red wine is exhibited like a work of art or an historical heirloom in the Smithsonian National Museum of American History in Washington, DC.

Winiarski has been a friend of mine for years. Born in 1928, he's a true hero of American winemaking. He grew up in a Polish neighborhood in Chicago and studied geology, political science, and agriculture, but it was a year spent studying in Naples and Tuscany that brought him to enology. His last name actually means something like "vintner" in Polish. He was an enologist at Robert Mondavi Winery before he began making his own wine in 1970. For years after the Judgment of Paris, Winiarski received letters from French winemakers viciously accusing him of having fixed the tasting.

In 2006, these three labels—Stag's Leap, Chateau Ste. Michelle, and Tignanello—began to sniff around each other and discuss possibly working together. What was most rewarding was that when Winiarski was ready to sell his legendary company and wanted to see it in good hands, he called me to find out whether I'd be interested. He offered out of friendship, sure, but also out of professional admiration. He's a fellow believer in family companies and in quality.

In 2007, the deal was completed: Antinori and Ste. Michelle are now the owners of Stag's Leap. Today we bottle S.L.V., which is aged for twenty-four months in French oak casks. But my favorite wine from Stag's Leap is Cask 23, an aromatic and elegant Cabernet that is only bottled in the best years.

Additional recognition of my work and my business philosophy came from the United States in early 2011, when Jess Jackson, founder and soul of one of California's other top wineries, Kendall-Jackson, passed away. Jackson created and grew his business in a relatively short time, using the best vineyards in the state, as well as other land in South America and in Tuscany's Chianti Classico region at Villa Arceno. The eulogy given at his packed funeral noted that the deceased's chief ambition in life had been to build "an

Antinori-type company." That was one of the loveliest honors I could receive.

We also share a great deal of mutual admiration with the Matte family, who own the Haras de Pirque estate in Maipo (Chile's version of Chianti, located between a river and hills). They not only make wonderful wine, but—to the delight of my daughters—also breed racehorses. Indeed, their cellar is horseshoe shaped. Thanks to a perfect combination of shoreline, hills, and flatlands, as well as clean air and wide-open spaces, Chile has produced exceptional reds for centuries. The first Chilean grapevines were planted near the town of La Serena sixty years before Christopher Columbus visited the area.

The wider world only took notice of Chile's exceptional wine-making in the 1990s, but there are already some who say that it offers the best wines anywhere. It combines perfect terroir with the best techniques from American and European wine companies. The French are particularly involved in Chile. They have even "cheated on" their usually sacred home ground and are exporting their knowledge (and their grapes). Our contribution to this emerging wine superpower is Albis, an intense red with aromas of currants and licorice that marries Cabernet Sauvignon with Chilean Carmenère grapes—a blended wine, and one of the first to combine different schools. I hope my daughters and my grandchildren will continue to develop it.

When people talk to me about the recession and tell me that globalization is hurting Italy, I often respond that we need to export know-how rather than goods and services. Intangibles such as experience, prestige, and tradition are our most precious resources. They are the raw materials that will ultimately help our economy recover. We need to focus on keeping quality high, too. Italians in general and Antinoris in particular have an innate tendency to seek high quality. My family's blue and yellow crest features friezes and cherubs and the Latin motto *Te duce proficio,* the pursuit of excellence. Earn. Grow. Improve.

Wine makes the world a better place. We really believe that. I grew up both as a man and as a businessperson in a world split into two political and economic blocks that both opposed each other and refused to communicate with each other. That all changed after the fall of the Berlin Wall in 1989. Among the many links in the chain that we've built across continents with our work, one of the most interesting is the Tuzko Bàtaapàti estate in Hungary. This wonderful Eastern-European vineyard has produced wine since the Roman era. It's located in one of the most long-standing wine-producing regions in Europe. For centuries, it supplied elegant white wines to the court of the Habsburgs and galas in the Austro-Hungarian Empire.

Then came Communism, the Soviet blockade, and collective farming. Wine was still made there, but it was industrial wine from enormous companies that harvested based on a predetermined calendar. Quantity won over quality. Wine doesn't care about politics, but it won't be rushed.

In the early 1990s, Hungary opened up to foreign investment. My friend Peter Zwack, from the youngest generation of a local family that had made bitters (including the very famous Unicum, a liqueur that contains forty different herbs), returned to Hungary in 1988, one year before Communism fell. He asked me to begin making good wine again in an area that had seen only grappa and liqueur for years, but we knew the whole business would have to be created from scratch.

My Italian partner, Jacopo Mazzei, and I began at the beginning. We traveled all over the country looking for a vineyard. We found land in the hills of Tolna, near the Danube, one hundred fifty kilometers south of Budapest. The ruins of ancient vineyards and cellars told us that grapes had once grown in the area. The gently hilly and green landscape seemed promising. It's early days yet. In 1991 we acquired the land, and since 2000 we've had complete control of the company. Today there are new vineyards and new cellars, and we're working with Chardonnay, Tramini, and Pinot Grigio grapes, but also with native grapes, including Kékfrankos, Bìborkadarka, and Kékoporto.

If we want to export that wine, we'll have to burnish the image of Eastern-European wines, which are still very misunderstood. I'm confident we can. Maybe these wines will lead us to the new markets in Asia, where there are entire societies that have yet to learn about wine. Today Russia, tomorrow China, later India. Different markets require different solutions, but basically we face the same obstacles my father did when he was trying to gain entry for his wines into the best restaurants in Rome and Naples. The same tools can be used to knock down cultural barriers and resistance: perseverance, impeccable quality, and reputation.

The winemaking company my ancestors founded today owns 1,742 hectares planted with vineyards in Italy, and 2,358 hectares around the world. Tuscany is our green heart, surrounded by a string of other vineyards from Piedmont to the north to Apulia to the south. A constellation of other new vineyards around the world is growing and gathering strength. We produce many bottles each year. Yet there are still new and exciting challenges to be met. For example, the humanitarian solidarity project in the UNESCO Biosphere in the province of Issyk-Kul, in the impoverished mountains of Kyrgyzstan, has really captured my imagination.

In 1999, Carl Hahn, former president of Volkswagen, asked me to work as a consultant on a farming project in Kyrgyzstan. The idea was to teach local populations modern craft techniques using local resources. The Swarovski crystal company and Loro Piana, maker of luxury Italian clothing, had already signed on. My family was asked to help launch wine production. We went to scout land for vineyards and found a perfect plateau with an altitude of 1,700 meters.

After I'd gone to check out the area, Albiera and Alessia visited four or five times, supervising right up until the first harvest. It would have been worth going just to see the expressions on the faces of the local Kyrgyzstan nomads as they witnessed two young Italian women — Alessia was only twenty-six or twenty-seven at the time — following the route traveled by Marco Polo. The vineyard was planted in an untamed spot on the shores of Issyk-Kul, one of the largest and widest lakes in the world. Because of its enormous volume of water, it has a tremendous effect on the microclimate of the entire mountain region.

As Albiera explained to me, people in this area had never heard of wine. So the first challenge was to explain the idea of a vineyard. Then we had to illustrate the concept of the harvest, wine cellars, fermentation. We planted Chardonnay, Riesling, and Pinot Noir grapes, which had to be covered in straw so they would survive the winter under half a meter of snow. Their ripening period is short but intense. And there were other new challenges to contend with: "The grapes had to be guarded at all times—the village came up with a schedule—otherwise they would have been stolen before they were fully ripe or while they were being transported," she said. "The locals had a hard time grasping the idea of an edible fruit that can't be eaten right away. In the end, though, the entire community put on a big celebration with bonfires, vodka, and sausages."

Today the vineyards and cellars in Kyrgyzstan provide a few dozen people with employment and a way to make a living, and they will for years to come, although things work a little differently there than they do back home. We've learned that bottles of wine are not sold for money there, but instead are bartered between families and with people in nearby towns in exchange for meat, seeds, and furs. Early civilizations did the same thing with the crops they grew. The vineyard may never produce an award-winning wine, but it's yielded some wonderful stories.

"Pure" *Vitis vinifera* appeared on earth for the first time in the middle of Asia, meaning that man first encountered this plant not far from our vineyard in Kyrgyzstan. The earliest signs of its cultivation were discovered in the Caucasus valleys, near what is now the border between Armenia and Turkestan, and they go back seven or eight thousand years. In 2007, in a cave in Armenia, a group of American archaeologists found a vat with traces of grape seeds that dates back about 6,100 years. Ancient winemakers are believed to have crushed the grapes with their feet. A stone tub for collecting the resulting juice was also found in the cave—a cool, dry place, like any good wine cellar.

The grapes there were probably the original *Vitis vinifera* that some paleobotanists believe can still be found in Asia. We may soon be able to create them in a laboratory. Because grapes are so important to human history, they are one of the few edible plants that have had their genome sequences mapped. The DNA of grapes was determined in 2007 by a team of French and Italian biologists—united, for once.

Anyone who's read Dante knows that in the Middle Ages, civilization developed in the direction of the sun, from east to west. Among the first to be enlightened were the ancient cities of Mesopotamia, followed by Egypt, Greece, and then Rome. The discovery of America supports this as well. And wine, a precious manifestation of human civilization, was born in the mountains of Asia and then refined by the Greeks. The Romans brought wine to all the lands they conquered, from North Africa to Germany. The Gauls and the Iberians, that is, the French and the Spanish, made wine an art and an obsession. Over the centuries, there have been great wines from the United States, Chile, Argentina, South Africa, Australia, and New Zealand.

I like to think that one day, when all the temperate zones of the Earth have been explored in the eternal search for the best terroir, someone will grow grapes professionally in the Caucasus, where it all began. When that happens, when the whole planet has been tested, we will know that the potential of every piece of land suitable for growing grapes has been tapped. I'm sure that somewhere, an Antinori will raise a glass to herald that event.

7

MEZZO BRACCIO MONTELORO

Opening a Winery

*E*arly word from the enologists is that Mezzo Braccio has notes of orange and elderberry. It envelops the palate and provides just a hint of yellow peach. It's one of our newest wines, made for the first time in 2007. It's Tuscan, and I've been watching it closely. It's not aged in barrels, so the essence of its terroir reaches the palate and the nose unfiltered. This wine is made on a hill in a vineyard north of Florence, five hundred meters above sea level in the foothills of the Apennines outside Fiesole.

For about ten centuries, Florentines have flocked to this cool, breezy area in the summer. Dante considered it paradise and is said to have come here with Beatrice. I find it interesting that one of our most advanced Italian experiments is taking place on land that is just short of mountainous. On this land, olive groves, small churches, wooded areas, charming villas, and aqueducts that date back to the Medici era abound, as do crystal-clear springs. After surveying the land and the microclimate, we began planting this estate in 2002 with Rhine Riesling, Pinot Bianco, Pinot Grigio, Sauvignon, and Gewürztraminer, and in a few years I expect to have an exceptional and unique wine. The 2007 vintage was good, but Mezzo Braccio has not come close to fulfilling its potential yet. As always, we need to be patient. The goal is exciting: The first high-quality white wine intended to age and improve over the years, made with international (mostly Northern European) grapes on Florentine soil. The fulfillment of a dream more than two generations old.

The altitude is noteworthy: five hundred meters is pretty high for a vineyard. Personally, I'm fascinated by winemaking in mountainous areas. Farmers are increasingly moving into those areas due to their pure air and cool climates. For decades now, the climate has been changing, and the atmosphere and the oceans have been warming. I won't get into the causes or the development of this global emergency, but I will say that grapevines are stubborn plants with much the same life expectancy as humans; like us, they're trying to find a way to deal with global warming, and they may be doing so by climbing higher toward the sky.

I've observed and admired high-altitude winemaking as it is practiced abroad and in Italy—in the Val d'Aosta region, in Spain, and in the Argentine Andes. In Italy, five hundred meters is traditionally considered the highest altitude viable for a vineyard, but in the Andes grapes are regularly grown at more than one thousand meters above sea level. By looking skyward, the Argentines were able to produce wine in the province of Salta, which is the same distance from the equator as Baghdad. I'm not talking about "emergency wines" created to quench the thirst of the enormous internal market, either, but about wines that are improving season after season and one day may even be given a featured spot on the shelves of our own *enoteche*.

Making wine at high altitude is a challenge for sure, but a rewarding challenge. It requires inventing new farming systems. Nights and early mornings are colder up that high, and that's a good thing, but it also means there are unexpected early frosts in the fall and late spring. And the more direct sunlight helps with photosynthesis, but it needs to be monitored closely so that the resulting wine isn't imbalanced. You need to take a long-term approach in this new area for high-quality winemaking, as in everything having to do with wine. You need to focus on the future, and you need to start experimenting now to find the right recipe further down the road.

Beyond this exploration of new habitats, a focus of our work as a company and as a family today is to seek out the best terroir that is already in use. We want each site where grapes are grown to realize its full potential. With an eye to that, we've worked on a four-year European Union program for the study and development of both widely used and largely abandoned native grapes. The list starts with the one hundred eighteen local Tuscan subspecies considered close to extinction. And with the same goal in mind, we've "spilled over" the borders of the original Tuscany/Umbria area and now work in other historic wine regions as well.

Since 1989, we've owned Prunotto, a company in the Langhe area of the Piedmont region, in the shadow of the Alps. We acquired Prunotto through Whitbread, and when I regained control of my company in the late 1990s, I made sure that Prunotto would stay in our hands. My daughter Albiera has been overseeing it for several years. Wine was made in Piedmont ten centuries before the birth of Christ. The Celts made that wine, and it was mixed with elderberry seeds and blackberries. This northern people brought wooden casks to Italy about two thousand five hundred years before Tignanello. Then came the Romans. The Savoy family—the Turin dynasty that later set off the movement for Italian unity—were among the first to make wine a status symbol, transforming the role of grape juice from opiate and medicine for the masses to a product for educated consumers with taste. In the mid-1500s, the Savoys had sommeliers at court. In the early 1900s, the members of Italy's royal family may still have spoken dialect in private, but when they dined they aspired to exhibit the same fine taste as the great monarchies of Europe. Their sommeliers served two different categories of wine: a *vino da bocca,* or palatable wine, reserved solely for the reigning family's dukes, and a different selection for any other guests who happened to be present.

The Savoys were interested in local grapes, cellars, and new winemaking technology. While they were in power in the eighteenth and nineteenth centuries, the entire region of Piedmont became a large-scale wine laboratory, and Barolo became known as "the wine of kings and the king of wines." Barbaresco, too, achieved a reputation for quality and prestige, due largely to the work of savvy producer Angelo Gaja. Piedmont was also the birthplace of Vermouth (an aromatized and fortified wine) and Barolo *chinato,* aromatized with local herbs, which farmers in the Langhe area used to cure anything that ailed them. The winemaking school in Alba and the Subalpine Agrarian Association were the first organizations of their kind in Italy and were both formed in Piedmont. The latter took as its motto the words of Alphonse de Lamartine: "It is not only wheat that emerges from the plowed earth, it is an entire civilization."

Piedmontese and Tuscan wines have always gone head-to-head in Italy. These two regions have much in common, including fiercely proud winemakers with strong ties to their land and a slew of prize-winning wines made from traditional grapes. Yet combining these two worlds with their own distinct histories was not easy. However, judging based on the final product, it was well worth the effort.

Alfredo Prunotto created the Prunotto winery about a century ago, but until we took over, Prunotto made wine from grapes grown elsewhere in the region, because it didn't have its own farmland. We began to create a network of selected vineyards that continued to grow. This proud company would be our launchpad for exploring and beginning to shape the perfect terroir for the area's local wines, but it was actually in bare-bones shape when we bought it. There, we've gotten familiar with legendary Piedmontese varieties, such as Nebbiolo, Barbera, and Dolcetto. With the idea that two heads are better than one, we worked with local producers, relying on our experience and their specific knowledge of the site. The result? The Costamiole vineyard in Agliano for Barbera d'Asti, the Bussia vineyard for Barolo, the Calliano vineyard for Albarossa and Syrah, and five hectares of Bric Turot in the Barbaresco area, plus five more in Treiso for Moscato.

We began working in the Apulia region in 1998 under the Tormaresca label in the region's Murgia and Alto Salento areas. This was another case—maybe even the best example—of redeeming marvelous terroir. Wine has been made on the plateaus of the "heel" of the Italian boot since the time of the ancient Romans. Until just a few years ago, this region was the largest producer of wine grapes in the entire country. However, most of the grapes were exported. As soon as they were cut from the vines, they were sent elsewhere in Italy and around the world, where they were used to make table wine.

Indeed, Apulia—which sits between the Adriatic and the Ionian—has long been known for quantity, not quality. That's been changing recently, and local terroir is now experiencing a true renaissance. Apulia is crisscrossed by wine routes, and modern wineries are popping up all over the region. Wines like Primitivo di Manduria, Negroamaro, Malvasia, and Aglianico are once again being recognized. There are twenty-five DOC wines in Apulia today. We hoped to make our own contribution to this fruitful and fertile movement.

A vacation-cum-exploration trip to this southern frontier opened our eyes to its potential. In the mid-1990s, I traveled there, Cotarella by my side, as always. It was immediately clear to us that though this region had a proud history and ancient grapes that dated back to the days of Magna Grecia, it had yet to blossom fully in enological terms. In many other places, Antinori has arrived and started out by selecting and reworking the grapevines and grooming the land. In Apulia, we found the inverse situation: wonderful grapes growing on perfect land, but an almost complete lack of modern facilities designed to produce high-quality wine.

Cantina di Masseria Maime has been in business since 2009. It's very modern and was conceived based on Renzo Cotarella's latest winemaking theories. It sits amid fields, woods, and centuries-old olive groves. We've worked on marketing, too, with innovations like Fichimori, a red wine meant to be served cold. We also make an extra-virgin olive oil from Cellina and Coratina olives, both native to Apulia.

Our projects in Piedmont and Apulia are signs of the times. At conferences and Q-and-A sessions, I'm inevitably asked how Italian businesses can be more competitive in a global market. I always give the same answer: we need to work together, using teamwork and networking. Piedmont and Tuscany's long-running winemaking rivalry, complete with closely guarded trade secrets and sniping, is an excellent example of the kind of deeply Italian provincial situation that has no place in the modern world.

The Italian wine business would never have survived the crisis of the 1960s if it hadn't invested in research and selection of raw materials; today, it will have no future if it doesn't engage in greater cooperation. In a free society in the global market, ideas circulate. They bump against each other without time or space barriers—new methods of communication have eradicated those. Ideological divides and pointless enmity between wine superpowers no longer make sense, whether we're talking about France versus Italy or California versus Chile.

As for technical issues, disputes over whether it's proper to age in barriques or not, or whether autochthonous grapes or traditional grapes are the right choice, have become meaningless. And it no longer makes any sense to keep secrets. It's time for the classic wine regions like Tuscany and Piedmont to work with the emerging regions like Apulia and Sicily, and even outliers like Sardinia and Abruzzo. Know-how and resources should circulate freely. That goes for grapes, but also for marketing and distribution methods.

France and the newer wine countries have always done things in an orderly way. In Italy, however, the wine world is fragmented and diffuse. There are a few large brands, and around those orbit nebulae of small, fragile companies subject to the volatility of the markets and defenseless against increasingly aggressive international competition. Fortunately, there's change afoot. The future will be full of small companies and high-quality estates, new labels and new players that are better connected through associations and consortia, with clear rules and recognizable and well-defined symbols to protect them. For example, today we've got the Istituto del Vino Italiano di Qualità Grandi Marchi, which has nineteen Italian company members from Piedmont to Sicily. I've been honored to serve as its president since it was founded eight years ago.

In that role, I think often of the late Pino Khail, who set an excellent example in cooperation until his passing in 2011.

I first met Khail in the 1970s, when a group of producers in Italy created the Unione Vini Italiani di Pregio. That organization's mission was to promote high-quality Italian wine. Piedmont's Fontanafredda, Verona's Bolla, our company and Ricasoli from Tuscany, Apulia's Rivera, and Sicily's Corvo di Salaparuta all participated. Pino Khail had a small advertising agency in Trieste at the time, and he handled our communications.

When the association was a few years old, I realized it was time to shake up our communications strategy. Rather than doing traditional advertising—something I've never been crazy about—I thought we should create a magazine about wine. The group agreed, and we held a meeting at Fontanafredda and told Khail what we planned to do—and that we would no longer require his services. He thought for a moment, and then he said, "If you want to create a wine magazine, I can do it for you. I've got the skills to do that." And so *Civiltà del Bere* was born. At first, the magazine was supported by the association, and then it became independent, including financially independent.

But Pino Khail was more than just the editor of a wine magazine. If one day someone writes a history of the last forty years in Italian wine—I suggest *The Italian Wine Renaissance* as a title—entire chapters will be dedicated to Khail. One of his many outstanding qualities was an ability to muster his charisma to foster teamwork in a business that had long been divided. He was able to vanquish mistrust and old rivalries and organize various members to stage promotions and tastings all over the world. Basically, he was the first person to instill team spirit among wine producers in Italy.

His finest hour came when he managed to get two great wine personalities who had different roots, politics, and ideas about wine to join the group and travel the world together. The first was Communist senator Walter Sacchetti, a native of Romagna and the longtime president of Riunite in Reggio Emilia. (Riunite was the producer of the Lambrusco that sold upwards of 200 million bottles a year in the United States and allowed its importer, the Mariani brothers' Banfi, to invest part of its profits in a huge winemaking project in Montalcino under the knowledgeable and enlightened direction of another important figure, enologist Ezio Rivella.) The second personality was Christian Democrat senator Paolo Desana, a Piedmont native and the first chairman of the Comitato Nazionale Vini di Origine. Sacchetti and Desana were like Peppone and Don Camillo: they fought constantly over politics and ideology, but deep down they were great friends. Their love of wine bonded them.

Pino Khail did all this with modesty, style, refinement, and, above all, great passion for wine. His death was a devastating loss for the business.

In short, if you can keep an open mind and let go of provincial attitudes, there are still regions to discover and new varietals to try in Italy. There are so many variables in one year in the life of a grape—a specific variety with a specific terroir and production philosophy—that it will always be different from any other produced anywhere in the world. The vintage of a wine is a story unto itself, written by the winemaker and by uncontrollable factors. Because of that, I'll never get tired of wine, and the pursuit of the perfect wine will never come to an end.

Back in Tuscany, in the Maremma area, there's one more new project that I've been following closely. There's a vineyard in Guado al Tasso called Matarocchio, where we've been producing Cabernet Franc for a few years. In 2007, we made three thousand bottles that have just gone on sale. It may turn out to be an unicum, a wine created only once before the grapes are then used for other things. Or this could be the start of an ongoing project.

Those wonderful 2007 grapes and that small plot of land really hit me hard; they are my latest enological crush. Sometimes I fall in love with a vineyard. It happened with the California hills for Antica and it happened with Solaia. The potential for a well-structured wine that will stand out from the crowd with sweet tannins and spicy notes simply overwhelms me in those moments.

I've been making wine for almost seventy years, if you count the bottle I made out of haphazardly assembled grapes with Professor Garoglio when I was still in short pants. But Matarocchio proves that my region's wine and land and my work can still surprise me and teach me something new.

Tuscany and the Tuscan way of doing things—a combination of taste, sensitivity, and a feeling of belonging that form the core of what it means to be an Antinori—are constants. They remain unchanged over time, despite fluctuating fashions. Tuscan passion underlies everything from farming to literature, from art to ritual. It informs even the mundane. The fact that our small Chianti company is now known around the world as one of the largest and most varied collections of vineyards has not changed that. We are Tuscans and Florentines. We are enterprising and creative people who love their work. We have continued to demonstrate and highlight our attachment to our region in recent years.

We're known on the streets of New York and Hong Kong, but Via Tornabuoni is our street. That's where our palazzo stands and where the chapel of my ancestors is located. I didn't hesitate recently when invited to lend my name and join a group of Florentine businesspeople who are interested in saving this ancient and elegant street from a state of disrepair. Just a few meters from our front door on Via Tornabuoni is Procacci, a Florentine institution that sells truffle sandwiches that are the perfect accompaniment to a glass of good wine.

Procacci was founded in 1885 by Leopoldo Procacci. The truffle sandwiches it sells were served at the court of King Victor Emanuel III and were graced with the royal seal. Everybody we know goes to Procacci. You can learn a lot more about Tuscan character from a visit to Procacci than you would from an academic paper or an encyclopedia entry. By 1997, operating costs had gotten so high (globalization hasn't done any favors for small, traditional businesses) that this little shrine to local flavors was on the verge of closing. It hadn't been handed down within the Procacci family, so we jumped at the chance to take it over. We kept the name and the style down to the last detail, including the early twentieth-century bar and windows, and we saved it from extinction. In 2006, we opened a branch of Procacci in Vienna, and in 2010 in Singapore.

Another place to experience a taste of Tuscany is our Cantinetta, a wine bar and restaurant that my father established in our palazzo in the 1950s. There are branches now around the world. Then there's our osteria at the estate in Badia a Passignano. Created in 2000 by Marcello Crini and managed with tender care by my daughter Allegra, the osteria has earned a Michelin star. Every day it offers up the tastes of the Antinori world on its menu. It serves our Cinta Senese pork from animals raised by Allegra in the Bolgheri brush in Bruciato. It serves oil that we produce in Tuscany, Umbria, and Apulia. The bread on the tables is made from our own organic flour; the vinegar is made from high-quality wine in small batches.

And, naturally, the wine list offers a full spectrum of Antinori wines. A kitchen is like a wine cellar—chefs need to be pushing constantly to grow and improve. The team of young chefs led by Matia Barciulli does just that. Tourists come from all over the world to take cooking classes. They learn to make breaded veal sweetbreads and fish lasagna with wild asparagus and bittersweet tomatoes. Then they participate in wine tastings and they shop in the store (the only place we sell our oldest vintages). They finish up with a visit to our ancient stone cellars.

In recent years, our brand has begun to expand beyond wine, though still with an emphasis on Tuscan classics: oil, country inns, restaurants, stores. This is new for us, and my daughters are heavily involved. I don't know where all these projects will lead, but we make sure that everything we do is in some way wine related and relies on those values that are so dear to the Antinori style: quality, Tuscan identity, tradition.

Today, many brands fall into the trap of diversifying too much, and in doing so they risk diluting their impact and images. Our family name is more than just a sales pitch. It does much more than flicker past on a stock exchange ticker. You won't find it on the packaging of souvenirs that are made in China. Ours is the last name of a family that lives with it every day. I'm always open to new Antinori businesses, but in the end, country inns and restaurants, cheeses and jams must be vehicles for and footnotes to the central aspect of our business: High-quality wine. Wine that is either Tuscan or is made in some other part of the world with Tuscan passion and dedication.

There is still room to delve deeper into the roots of our identity as Tuscan vintners, and we have no intention of abandoning our exploration of new areas and new formulas. The future of wine will be written by the dialogue between these two approaches. Ancient and autochthonous grapes will continue to be refined through selection and vineyard work. International grapes will continue to explore the biosphere in search of new territory. There's an entire planet waiting for seeds to be sown, plants to be nurtured and trimmed, grapes to be harvested, and so on through the entire cycle.

Exciting new things are happening with sparkling wine in southern England. In 2006, sparkling wine from the Ridgeview estate in East Sussex was served at Buckingham Palace to commemorate the eightieth birthday of Queen Elizabeth II. Plenty of English people adore a good Bordeaux or a Tuscan wine, so I can imagine what that meant to them. There was a time when no one in Scotland would have considered growing grapes or drinking anything local other than beer and whiskey, but Scotland, too, recently produced its first high-quality wine in Ardeonaig on Tay Lake between the Highlands and the North Sea. That wine went on sale in 2010.

For the sake of the future, we need to be present and active in many places. We need to follow up on every lead and always be on the lookout for ways to spur on and guide changes in wine's image and the way wine is used. Consumers will ultimately determine our new production styles, the language we speak, and the direction our experimentation will take. The grapevine (pun fully intended) of the Italian and international markets is buzzing with encouraging and interesting signs.

Lallo—the cellar master who disdained all wine but the local Chianti—is long gone, and there's no turning back to those days. Tuscans don't restrict themselves to drinking Tuscan wine, and the people of Piedmont drink wine from outside the Langhe area. Australian, American, South African, Chilean, and Croatian wines are no longer a novelty. That's a good thing. "Loyalty" has no place in wine; it simply causes people to cut themselves off from interesting possibilities. Wine is pleasure, and pleasure is born of curiosity and the desire to make new discoveries.

Fish is more frequently paired with red wine? Fine, let's give it a try. Various ethnic cuisines are increasingly common in our homes and out at restaurants. And why not? It's exciting to figure out the best wine to pair with curry, or couscous, or spring rolls.

I'm highly interested in modern distribution. I see an informed public made up of conscious consumers, including even the youngest consumers. The number of wine bars is growing, so there are more spaces for informal tastings. The Internet is full of places to discuss wine. Wine is increasingly accessible. In Italy, even large-scale distributors are changing. I keep an open mind about all of it. As long as the person selling wine knows how to display it, transport it, and explain it to the consumer, I have no problem with it. As long as there's passion and respect for wine, any place and any tool that introduces it to the largest number of people will work.

With this demand for quality and this new focus on materials, the revolutionary thing to do will be to produce fewer wines, but better wines, though that may take decades. We've seen that wine can go up the mountain to discover new countries and new continents, but it can't be made everywhere. *Vitis vinifera* must be treated properly to yield an honest product. It needs sun in the summer, rain, cold in the winter; it suffers if it is grown too far outside of temperate zones, or it never feels a sea breeze, or it is transported to areas where the seasons don't change. Grapes don't fare well in humid summers, and they detest smog and cement. Their habitat can't be changed completely. And unlike genetically modified wheat or apricots grown in greenhouses, grapes can't be harvested more than once a year. Nor can you hurry a grapevine and force it to produce fruit before its time. You'll never get good quality that way.

So wine is and always will be a renewable resource, but not an inexhaustible one. If one day the masses in China, India, and Brazil want to enjoy a glass, winemakers will still need to stick to the idea of fewer wines of higher quality. In traditional winemaking areas like Italy, it will be increasingly rare to have wine on the table every day, but on the right occasion, consumers will educate themselves much more than today's average wine drinkers do, and they'll be looking for a bottle that offers an experience and sensory emotion. They'll look for something new, something better. And wine will increasingly be available in places where today it is unknown if not unattainable: India, China. Places that have not seen wine splash out of a tap and into a carafe. There will be less demand for mass-market wine, table wine with no certification, the kind of wine my ancestors made that was intended to quench thirst and nothing more. That kind of mass-market wine isn't good—not for your health, not for your waistline, and not for the Earth.

So what will people buy? What kind of wine will be popular in the coming decades of this century? High-quality Italian wine is still key. I don't think there will be some big revolution. Wooden barrels at first were mysterious and then gradually came to be accepted and are now widely used (even a little too widely). Now they're just another tool available to winemakers. Vino novello was a hot trend in the 1980s and 1990s, though it's currently falling out of favor. Today, people want more aged wines with strong links to terroir and tradition. Wines with a history that age gracefully. Their character comes from those who work in the vineyards and the respect they have for the soil.

For all these reasons, wine will be an increasingly natural product. Quality will be achieved within the parameters of environmental friendliness. There will be ever more studies on soil and chemistry. Genetic improvements will come, too, as we learn more and more about the microbiological processes that lead to good wine. Other microbiological processes will be banished, however— I'm talking about chemical shortcuts for fertilization, speeding up the process, altering colors and flavors. Those will disappear. The market is going to demand that.

Natural materials such as glass, cork, wood, paper, and cardboard will be used for growing, storing, packaging, and distribution. They'll be diligently recycled. Our wineries and the other places where wine is made will respect the landscape and its life cycle. They'll use sun and natural light and conserve water. All the parts of the grapevines that are not used to make wine will be recycled and used as sources of green energy.

There's a project that ties together many threads that have run through the last century and have been mentioned in this book, and connects them as a single strand to the future of wine: the family and Tuscany, vineyards outside of Italy's borders, and ecological wineries. I'm referring to Biserno and the wine that company produces. Created in the early 2000s, Biserno is my brother, Lodovico's project and a new venture for both of us. I'm the older brother, and I was handed the reins of the company. I've helped it grow and made it stronger. But Lodovico, too, has worked in New York, in London, and in the Maremma vineyards, and has represented our family name and our wine well. My Tignanello is one tile in our great mosaic. His Ornellaia is another sign of our pride and creativity.

In any case, both of us want to make great wine. The time has come for us to do it together. (That's not the only thing we do together, either. We love spending time with our children and grandchildren as a family, and we love talking about wine and sports. As we once told an audience of journalists, he thinks he skis better than I do, but I know I play a better game of golf than he does.)

This story takes us back to Tuscany once more, near my father's and my mother's vineyards. We began this journey with three vineyards along the road between Bolgheri and Bibbona, where Tuscan wine became great. This is the birthplace of Insoglio del Cinghiale, a 35 percent Syrah wine that incorporates carefully inspected French grapes. Biserno, modeled after the great Bolgheri wines, arrived in 2006.

But today's vintners have a new vision and different boundaries. Lodovico and his enologist, Helena Lindberg, decided it was time to look at land very far away. The Sauvignon Blanc grapes for this new wine grow at the feet of the Wither Hills near Marlborough, New Zealand, in an alluvial valley perfect for wine. When the news broke of our arrival in the area, local winemaking guru Brent Marris commented, "He chose the best spot in the entire region to plant grapes. These Tuscan brothers really know their wine!"

The first grapes in the area were planted by an Anglican pastor two hundred years ago, when we had already sold bottles and flasks at Palazzo Antinori for four centuries. High-quality wines have only been made there for about fifteen years, but various experts believe the soil in the land that the Maori call Aotearoa, which sits closer to the Antarctic than any other inhabited land, is perfect for white wine. I would never have dreamed of such a thing, but you have to be ready to adjust your outlook at all times. As in California, as in Chile, you can understand what land can provide for wine only if you work that land side by side with its winemakers, and only after you have lived through a few harvests. Since 2007, Mount Nelson Ram's Hill Sauvignon Blanc has been made in Marlborough. It's sold directly to some of the world's best restaurants, and it pairs perfectly with sushi.

We're nearly fifteen years into the new millennium, and the world is changing quickly. My daughters, my colleagues, and I are ready. We'll continue to make wine with the best raw materials, the best technology, and our broad base of knowledge, without ever losing sight of our roots and our tradition. We're fortunate to have the manpower to pursue this mission in many places at once.

I have one last story to tell you, this one set halfway between our Tuscan roots and the wine of the future. It's a story about a hill. A few years ago, Lodovico said, "The French have châteaux? Wine castles? We'll fill our countryside with the cellars of famed winemakers." He was riffing on what my father said when he was searching for a name for his first new wine and threw down the gauntlet to Bordeaux and the world and said, "They have châteaux, but we have villas." That was in the late 1920s, on the cusp of great change; we're again on the cusp of great change in the second decade of the 2000s.

San Casciano Val di Pesa is the historic heart of the Marchesi Antinori wineries. My grandfather Piero had the first facilities for winemaking and for aging wines built there. They were large, efficient, and convenient to town. It was a great idea—modern for its time. Dr. Charlemagne's bottles of poorly fermented sparkling wine exploded there, between the San Casciano Val di Pesa residential area and an oak and beech forest, just on the other side of the Pesa River, the natural border of the Chianti Classico area. There, too, the automatic weapons of the retreating Germans fired on the day when I got my first inkling of what I wanted to do with my life.

For fifty years, our bottles have been shipped from there all over the world. First the bottles were washed and dried. Then they were filled by generations of workers. Women glued on the labels one at a time, and then, finally, they were crated, using one of the early conveyor-belt systems. A small forest of wine tanks from different eras and in different materials and of different sizes stands rusting around the buildings. In San Casciano in the first half of the last century we collected the best Chianti Classico grapes (after my grandparents and my father had contracted with brokers), and then transformed them into liters and liters of excellent wine. Those wines have been tasted and praised—and sometimes decried—at grand wine tastings held in rooms with tie-beam ceilings by thousands of wine journalists who write in various languages and adhere to various schools of thought. We've shipped and spread those aromas and flavors—in boxes of six, in demijohns, kegs, and cases—everywhere from Florence to Montevideo, from Moscow to Toronto.

This is the place where five centuries after the first Antinori wine was made, winemaking became our business. Palazzo Antinori on the Piazza Antinori in Florence is the address where our importers and distributors send packages, letters, and telegrams. Our "Florentine château" anchors us to our identity, even as the world spins ever faster. There, as I write, conduct meetings, and talk on the telephone, I'm surrounded by memories of my ancestors. Overhead are wooden beams inlaid by Giuliano da Maiano, the architect who worked in the style of Brunelleschi; Lorenzo de' Medici recommended my ancestors hire him to finish building their house.

I step into the courtyard to get a breath of fresh air and amid the gray stone, the red bricks, the white plaster, and the dark wood, all under the shade of a large magnolia tree, my thoughts wander. This is our stronghold on the Arno River, lost for decades and reclaimed by my father. For centuries, my ancestors gathered in these rooms—often seated around a table—to discuss Florentine politics and European trade routes. They invited judges and prelates and generals and royalty to dinner and poured them glasses of Chianti and conducted business. This building and the Val di Pesa cellars are a tangible representation, walls that support who are and who we were. Despite all this—maybe even because of all this—soon they will be no more, at least not in their current form.

We made the decision more than ten years ago, and we've never had so much trouble getting from concept to implementation. For some time, San Casciano has been too small. Designed a century ago and then renovated and expanded as our company has grown and changed, our home base in Tuscany became unmanageable and costly. The wine has to travel too far. There's little room to expand to keep up with the growing market. It has too many buildings that can no longer be adapted to new techniques and new technologies. The town of San Casciano Val di Pesa has grown around us and now barely tolerates the constant traffic as trucks and vans bring in grapes and take out bottles.

There are plans to build a ring road, a river of asphalt that will run just a few meters away from our Chianti Classico. It all boils down to this: the cellars aren't working for us anymore. By the time of this book's publication in English, they will have already produced their last bottles, and they will have been demolished, just as the castle in Combiate was, but peacefully. It was time to move. Our Florentine palazzo was also getting a little small, and it's increasingly complicated to run our wineries from the downtown of a busy city. We needed new offices. Change offers an opportunity for new beginnings. When one cycle ends, another starts. It's a form of spring cleaning. You get rid of preconceived notions and clear out the cobwebs. So we didn't just build new cellars and new offices. We created something completely different.

When you first see the hill carpeted in light green grapevines from the road, it looks like any other hill in the Chianti area. Then, you notice a horizontal line across the slope, like a smile or one of Lucio Fontana's slashes across a canvas made of grass. The new Antinori Chianti Classico winery in Bargino, in the municipality of San Casciano, but far from the residential area, was finished in 2013. The winery runs alongside the ancient Via Cassia, on the strategically important segment between Florence and Siena. It sits amid vineyards and olive groves, clad in *pietra serena,* a local gray sandstone. The rooms comprise a small underground kingdom, cellars in the form of a small city made of terra-cotta, marble, wood, and glass.

First we imagined our dream winery, and then we chose Florentine architect Marco Casamonti to build it. Casamonti, who's thirty years younger than I am, is the founder of the Archea Associati firm and creator, among other things, of the entrance to the fiftieth Venice Biennale. When we contacted him, he had just published a book called *Cantine,* or *Wine Cellars.* The book features the recent work of "starchitects" in Italy, as well as in France, Spain, and the United States. It speaks of the need for these revolutionary new structures to blend design and function, so that they serve as both symbols and workplaces and are in harmony with the landscape and nature.

One of the first times we met in person, Casamonti told me, "A wine cellar is an ambivalent space. It's a sacred and silent space, a temple to the ancient rites of the grape, but it's also a production area and as such needs to meet certain requirements. And today it has to be a rural building that is immersed in and in perfect harmony with nature—that's what makes these projects so fascinating and difficult." I was sold.

At that point, Albiera took charge of the project. Paolo Giustiniani of the Hydea firm helped with engineering, and Renzo Cotarella oversaw the technical aspects of the places where wine will be made. "It's been a lot of work," my daughter tells me, "even just the bureaucratic side, with the permits and authorization." She's something of an expert at this point, and the Bargino project has been her main focus for the last few years. "Then there's the issue of designing a workplace that doesn't damage the surrounding vineyards. There was a long hunt for the right materials. Just when things got going, part of the hill collapsed and we had to buttress the whole thing and make structural changes to reinforce the land. Then we started all over again from square one."

We used everything we learned about the world of wine—the new world of wine—in designing the Bargino winery. It has zero impact ecologically, and it doesn't disrupt the countryside visually. (The 37,000 square meters of space are almost invisible from the outside.) It uses natural light as much as possible. The entire complex is underground, including the parking areas. The materials are natural and Tuscan.

Visitors can tour any of our vineyards. We hold exhibits, musical events, festivals, and meetings at many of them. But this is the first large Antinori structure intentionally created for an audience. A wine audience. At the start, the tourists have been mostly foreigners, but I think soon Italians are going to grow dissatisfied with simply buying wine; they'll want to get to know it better and learn about how it's made. This is a cultural trend that began in California, arrived in France, and finally in Italy has given rise to wine itineraries, enological museums, and a small creative revolution in the form of these stylized cellars, the kind featured in Casamonti's book and referenced by my brother, Lodovico.

These kinds of wineries have cropped up in the last ten years, largely in Maremma. They are modern, efficient, and ecofriendly buildings that are not just places for making and selling great Tuscan wines. Instead, they are themselves works of art—small monuments to Italian enology and creativity. They are the linchpins of a new marketing model for a Tuscany that has become a brand of its own, a high-quality product.

Swiss architect Mario Botta designed a harmonious stone and brick "open cask" on one of the San Lorenzo hills near Suvereto for Petra's three-hundred-hectare estate. Brescia businessman Vittorio Moretti, who created the excellent Petra Val di Cornia (his daughter Francesca now runs the vineyard—she's part of the new wave of women in wine), commissioned it.

Another example is the new home of the Rocca di Frassinello winery in the Grosseto area, owned by our friend, publisher Paolo Panerai. This one was designed by Renzo Piano, Genoa's answer to Brunelleschi and the architect behind the Centre Pompidou in Paris and The New York Times building. Piano designed a tower, a red clay parallelepiped that's partially underground. As in all the newly designed wineries (and many of Antinori's recent establishments), the grapes are transported to the winemaking area naturally, carried by gravity. A plaza around the tower hosts events and welcomes visitors. Below ground there is an enormous aging area full of casks.

In Castagneto Carducci, Ambrogio Folonari and his son, Giovanni, are building a winery/museum of wood, glass, and clay at their Campo di Mare estate. It was designed by Jean-Michel Wilmotte, who created several wings for the Louvre in Paris.

And in Maremma, Piedmontese architect Giovanni Bo's design for Ca' Marcanda is allowing the Angelo Gaja family—one of the standard-bearers in Langhe area wines—to launch itself in Tuscany. The structure comprises buildings of varying sizes, partially underground, that peek out from between the olive trees.

Finally, there's Lodovico's new winery at the Campo di Sasso estate. Lodovico said, "Architecturally significant Tuscan wineries that project an air of seriousness and elegance and are mindful of the environment can help create an identity that further distinguishes the region." Milanese architect and designer Gae Aulenti was behind this stark, linear project in the Maremma area, which will sit largely underground, just steps from the cypress-lined roads of Bolgheri. There, with the help of French star enologist Michel Rolland, my brother and I will produce and age two new wines: Pino di Biserno and Biserno.

The Bargino winery is something else. It is the first of its size and is able to handle very large numbers of visitors. Our visitors will have a chance to see, study, and touch the places where wine is made, the laboratory where we construct our barrels, a small nursery, and the vin santo cellars. They will follow the process of making wine, from the unloading of the grapes at the start to the tanks to the cellars where in the dark in ten thousand barrels, grape must is transformed into Chianti Classico. There are family heirlooms and mementoes, as well as items from the history of winemaking and other works of art. For the wine museum, we've amassed a collection of prints depicting hunting and winemaking, and one of the highlights is a fantastic press that dates to the Renaissance and was designed by no less a genius than Leonardo da Vinci.

Chianti Classico and other top Tuscan wines are living, breathing entities at Bargino. Walking over bridges and gazing through the windows, wine lovers are treated to the sight of the tanks where grape must ferments, but also an olive mill, an oven for baking bread, and many, many bottles—a kind of glass and cork archive of all the wines we've ever made. The wine ages underground as it always has. Each step of the process takes place in a cool area sheltered from direct sunlight. I've written that rivalries between winemakers no longer make any sense. This new winery is entirely transparent. Everyone will see what we do—a concept I learned from my friend Mondavi in California—so that the wine is created in an open environment, where both air and ideas circulate freely.

It is a modern temple to Chianti Classico and our family history in the heart of our land. The company headquarters and offices that are connected to the world markets have also moved here from Palazzo Antinori. As long as I'm alive and able, I'll work here with my daughters and my coworkers. The buildings are invisible from the outside, but from a large terrace with a view I'll be able to look out over my land and my vineyards.

We're not running away. Our stone building in Florence will continue to serve as a site for conferences and tastings; we'll still run the Cantinetta on the ground floor. But it's time for a change. Time to create a new home base for future generations of my family. With

Bargino, we're officially moving back to the country, to the place my ancestors were forced to leave eight hundred years ago. We're going back as businesspeople and vintners. Men and women from three generations, more united than ever. We'll begin to be less connected to Florence, and more connected to Chianti.

Like a good vineyard tended with love after investment, experimentation, and selection, this winery is a long-term project. It's impossible to know where it will take us. It is the crowning achievement of my career and my life as a winemaker. It is a place that represents me and speaks of my ideas about wine, land, Tuscany, the future. It is sophisticated but not invasive, new but made with ancient materials, as harmonious as a Renaissance dome, but also highly efficient. I'm reminded often of what my partner in enological adventure, Giacomo Tachis, wrote and said about the new trend in wineries as entertainment: "Go ahead and make your museum winery, but keep in mind that the land and the wine must always be at the center of everything."

What I like best about the new winery is this: the whole time people are there in certain areas, attending conferences, eating Tuscan food in a restaurant, listening to concerts in the auditorium, and purchasing bottles of wine, in other areas grapes are being destemmed, and at just the right moment the sweet juice of those grapes will be moved from vats to barrels, and then from barrels to bottles.

My father's Chianti Classico and Villa Antinori are the first to age in the cool air of the lowest floor of the complex, fifteen meters below ground, with their older brothers. And just a few scant meters of Chianti earth separate the offices and the museum from the surface above, where soil is weeded and fertilized, plants grafted, and fruit harvested.

Critics are already chattering about these "super wineries," Super Tuscan estates where vineyards grow above the roofs of the buildings. They've called them a great work of Tuscan art, part of a new Renaissance. They speak of them as if Machiavelli and Raphael were back among the living.

But when I look at our new winery, I see one thing above all: I see a wonderful place to make great wine.

TECHNICAL NOTES

MONTENISA BRUT ROSÉ
—— (First sold in 2003) ——

CLASSIFICATION: Franciacorta DOCG

GRAPES: 100 percent Pinot Nero

VINIFICATION: In early spring, after initial alcoholic fermentation that occurs partially in stainless-steel tanks and partially in barrels, the wine undergoes a second fermentation in the bottle and then remains in contact with yeasts for at least twenty-four months. The *remuage* is still performed by hand using the signature *pupitres* in the traditional manner, and each bottle receives great individual attention. After *dégorgement,* the bottles rest for at least three months before being released.

TASTING NOTES: The wine has a rosy pink color, creamy foam with subtle, lingering *perlage.* The aroma is clearly that of Pinot Nero, with notes that echo the particular features of the grape. Full-bodied, elegant, slightly acidic, fresh, and complex on the palate, due in part to prolonged contact with yeasts.

VILLA ANTINORI

— *(2007 vintage)* —

CLASSIFICATION: Toscana IGT

GRAPES: 55 percent Sangiovese, 25 percent Cabernet Sauvignon, 15 percent Merlot, and 5 percent Syrah

CLIMATE: The meteorological conditions during winter and spring, with above-average temperatures, caused vegetative regrowth to take place quite early in the season. This also affected the phases of fruit setting and veraison. The significantly early progression of the vegetative cycle diminished as the season continued, due in part to the rain in the second half of August. September was characterized by good weather and dry conditions, which encouraged the perfect ripening of all the grape varietals, and enabled the harvest to be carried out at the right moment. Harvesting was initiated in early September with Merlot, followed by Syrah and Cabernet Sauvignon, and ended in early October with Sangiovese.

VINIFICATION: After being destemmed and gently pressed, the grapes were transferred to temperature-controlled stainless-steel tanks. Alcoholic fermentation began the day after the pressing of the grapes and lasted for five to seven days, whereas maceration lasted from eight to twelve days, depending on the varietal. Fermentation temperatures never exceeded 30°C for Cabernet and Sangiovese grapes, in order to help ensure proper extraction of the color and the soft tannins. In the case of Syrah and Merlot, fermentation temperatures never exceeded 25°C, in order to preserve the aromatic components. The resulting wine underwent malolactic fermentation during the months of October and November, and afterward it was transferred to French, Hungarian, and American oak barrels for twelve months of aging. The wine was then bottled and left to age for another eight months.

TASTING NOTES: The wine has an intense ruby red color. It offers full and complex aromas that recall ripe fruit, plum jam, mint, chocolate, and tobacco. In the mouth, the wine presents itself with good body; it is round, with soft tannins. The finish is long and leaves hints of ripe fruit on the palate.

SOLAIA

—— (1997 vintage, Wine Spectator 2000 Wine of the Year) ——

CLASSIFICATION: Toscana IGT

GRAPES: 75 percent Cabernet Sauvignon, 5 percent Cabernet Franc, 20 percent Sangiovese

CLIMATE: The latter part of winter and the beginning of spring were very mild for the time of year and also very dry. This produced early budding—some ten days earlier than average. In April the temperature suddenly dropped, causing an arrest in the growth of the buds. The summer was very hot and sunny and this weather continued throughout all of September and for the duration of the harvest, which meant that the grapes were exceptionally healthy and had a high sugar concentration when picked. Overall, the 1997 harvest was a bit below expectations in terms of quantity, but in terms of quality, this is an exceptional vintage, probably even better than the much-acclaimed 1990 vintage and one of the best of the last fifty years.

VINIFICATION: The grapes from the Solaia vineyard, which are always selected according to strict criteria, were among the last to be harvested (starting September 22 for the Cabernet grapes, and a week later for the Sangiovese). The grapes were destemmed and pressed gently and vinified separately using new methods. Maceration took place in fifty-hectoliter open, wooden fermenters with periodic cap submersion for better extraction of color, complexity, and tannins. During this time (fifteen days for the Sangiovese and twenty days for the Cabernet), the wine completed its alcoholic fermentation without its temperature ever going above 30°C. The wine was then transferred into new and one-year-old barrels (from the Allier and Tronçais brand), where malolactic fermentation occurred by year's end. The wines were then racked, blended, and then returned to the barriques for about fourteen months of aging. They were then bottled and aged for an additional twelve months before release.

TASTING NOTES: The wine has a deep garnet color, and the aromas include leather, hay, black pepper, and blackberries and blueberries, with hints of mint and dark chocolate. It has good structure and is well-balanced, with soft, silky tannins and a lingering finish. It is complex yet retains the strong and straightforward character typical of its region.

TIGNANELLO

— (1975 vintage) —

CLASSIFICATION: Toscana IGT (Val di Pesa table wine)

GRAPES: 90 percent Sangiovese, 10 percent Cabernet Sauvignon and Cabernet Franc

CLIMATE: Climate as a whole was seasonal. The spring season was good, although there were some unexpected frosts. A long, hot summer led into a mild October. Grapes were carefully selected during harvest, since production was intended to be limited.

VINIFICATION: The grapes were handled separately. Maceration lasted for twelve days and the temperature was kept to 29°C or below. Malolactic fermentation followed and was completed on December 18. The wine was transferred to Allier and Tronçais French oak barrels and was kept there for eighteen months. It was then aged an additional fifteen months in bottles.

TASTING NOTES: The wine is still in excellent condition in terms of both intensity and color. It has a welcoming aroma with hints of tobacco, wet hay, and spices. The tannins are well managed and the wine has a slightly vibrant and sweet finish. Its firm structure is intense and long lasting.

CERVARO DELLA SALA
— (1986 vintage) —

CLASSIFICATION: Umbria white table wine

GRAPES: 80 percent Chardonnay, 20 percent Grechetto

CLIMATE: Spring and the first half of summer were cool and some-what rainy. From mid-July onward, the climate was perfect for the grapes to ripen. As a result, at harvest time the grapes had excellent levels of sugar and acidity.

VINIFICATION: The grapes were harvested early in the morning and, after destemming, were macerated briefly (about ten hours) at a temperature between 3°C and 5°C. The must was then immediately separated from the skins and placed in 225-liter oak barrels in the Castello della Sala cellars. It underwent alcoholic fermentation for about twenty days. The wine then underwent malolactic fermentation and was left untouched until bottling in order to prolong contact with yeasts. The wine was in the French oak barrels (Allier, Tronçais, and Limousin) for six months in all. It was racked and bottled on site and then aged for an additional ten months in the cellars.

TASTING NOTES: The wine has a complex aroma with hints of minerals, fruits, and flint. It has a generous and savory palate that is in line with the aromas, with a mineral finish typical of this wine in particular. It's a well-balanced and refined wine—never heavy.

ANTICA NAPA VALLEY
—— (2004 vintage) ——

CLASSIFICATION: Atlas Peak District, Napa Valley

GRAPES: 100 percent Cabernet Sauvignon

CLIMATE: The climate was steadily warm and budding occurred early in the spring. There were some spikes in the temperature in late summer, and as a result the harvest was fifteen days earlier than it is on average—from September 27 to October 14, to be exact. The Cabernet Sauvignon grapes that resulted were small in size but fully ripe.

VINIFICATION: The grapes were harvested in the cool early-morning hours. They were destemmed, pressed, and subject to fermentation, a process that would last for ten days at a maximum temperature of 29°C. The wine was then transferred to new French oak barrels for malolactic fermentation, which was completed by December. The wine remained in the barrels for another twelve months, exposed to the open air as needed. In spring 2006, the wine was bottled and then aged in bottles for an additional twelve months.

TASTING NOTES: The wine is rich and concentrated with aromas of currants, plums, and sour cherries. The toasted oak flavor translates into hints of coffee. This is a well-balanced wine with a long-lasting finish, firm tannins, and a light mineral flavor. Its rich and concentrated fruit flavors make it an excellent candidate for aging.

MEZZO BRACCIO MONTELORO
— *(2009 vintage)* —

CLASSIFICATION: Toscana IGT

GRAPES: 100 percent Riesling

CLIMATE: The growing season began with a rather wet spring, which created a slight delay in the development of the vegetation but did not interfere with the regular growth of the plant. Ample reserves of ground water were, in fact, helpful in replenishing deeper levels below ground. This turned out to be quite useful during the summer, as July and August were hot and rather dry with extensive sunlight and high temperatures. The first rains in mid-September brought relief and assisted in preventing significant vine stress. Ripening began in early August and continued rather rapidly. The harvest began in late September, fifteen days earlier than in 2008.

VINIFICATION: Grapes were picked by hand from the sunniest vineyards. Riesling requires rapid ripening in order to accumulate the proper level of sugar without compromising its acidity. The grapes were destemmed and given a soft pressing to extract the juice as gently as possible. Fermentation was carried out entirely in stainless-steel tanks at temperatures that never exceeded 16°C. The various lots of Riesling were blended in April. In order to preserve aroma, the wine was then kept in stainless-steel tanks at a temperature of 10°C until bottling in early summer.

TASTING NOTES: The wine has clean and elegant aromas of fine complexity with candied apricots as the principal underlying note. The ripeness of the fruit lends sweetness on the palate, well sustained by a crisp, savory, and elegant acidity. There are classic notes of petroleum on the finish and aftertaste.